T0114614

Napolo and Other Poems

Copyright © Moira Chimombo 2021

All rights reserved. No part of this book may be reproduced, stored
in a retrieval system, or transmitted, in any form or by any means,
electronic, mechanical, photocopying, recording, or otherwise,
without prior written permission from the copyright holder.

First published 2009 by WASI Publications, Zomba

Luviri Press
P/Bag 201 Luwinga
Mzuzu

ISBN   978-99960-66-78-8
eISBN 978-99960-66-08-5

Back cover photograph by Moira Chimombo

Luviri Reprints no. 14

Napolo and other Poems

Steve Chimombo

Luviri Press

Mzuzu
2021

DEDICATION

To the sons and daughters of Napolo

By the Same Author

Poetry
Napolo Poems (Manchichi)
Napolo and the Python (Heinemann)
Epic of the Forest Creatures (WASI)
Breaking the Beadstrings (WASI)
Python! Python! (WASI)
The Vipya Poem (WASI)
Ndakatulo za Napolo (Manchichi)

Plays
The Rainmaker (Popular Publications)
Wachiona Ndani? (Dzuka)
Sister! Sister! (WASI)
Achiweni Wani? [translation of *Wachiona Ndani?*] (Manchichi)

Novels
The Basket Girl (Popular Publications)
The Wrath of Napolo (WASI)

Children's Literature
Caves of Nazimbuli (Popular Publications and Luviri))
Child of Clay (Popular Publications)
Operation Kalulu (Popular Publications and Luviri))
The Bird Boy's Song (WASI and Luviri))

Short Stories
Tell me a Story (Dzuka)
The Hyena Wears Darkness (WASI and Luviri)
Of Life, Love, and Death (WASI)

Folklore
Malawian Oral Literature (Center for Social Research and Luviri)
Napolo ku Zomba (Manchichi)

Criticism
The Culture of Democracy [with Moira Chimombo] (WASI)
AIDS Artists and Authors (WASI)

General
Directory of Malawian Writing (Dept of Arts and Crafts)

Acknowledgements

This is a collection of poetry from several sources. Some are from my own *Napolo Poems* (WASI, 1987) and *Napolo and the Python* (Heinemann, 1995); others from various anthologies: *Malawian Writing Today* (Malawi Pen, 1999), *The Unsung Song* (Chancellor College Publications, 2001), *Operations and Tears* (Kachere, 2003); and yet others from international publications: *Summer Fires* (Heinemann, 1983) and *Modern Poetry* (Penguin, 1986). Some poems have been gleaned from local periodicals like *Odi, Outlook, Nation*, and *WASI*; others from international ones: *The Malahat Review* (Canada, 1975) or *The Greenfield Review* (USA, 1979). All these received proper acknowledgements in their earlier appearances.

Table of Contents

Introduction

"Some of your poetry, 'Napolo' and 'Obituary,' for example, can be interpreted along the same political lines as those of others, whom we know suffered detention or exile during the Banda dictatorial regime," a reader once remarked. "How come, do you think, you managed to get away with your equally castigating poetry? You were never detained or exiled, or were you?"

"How did you survive the detention of writers during the one-party regime?" another asked.

These are some of the chastening reminders a writer goes through. My mind goes back to some of the instances when I was close to incarceration, death, or exile. I, too, wonder at how I managed to keep out of the clutches of Banda's minions. A few personal examples will suffice.

"My promotion depends on detaining people like you." This statement was addressed to me by a senior police officer at a popular place in the mid-1970s. It was packed with informers, Special Branch, drug and drink addicts, prostitutes, and the usual lay-byes. I had gone there for relaxation, to think about nothing in an atmosphere different from books and academic stuff. Almost anything could have happened there, though. The police officer telling me his career prospects on my incarceration was just one of the happenstances of the place, if not the country, then.

At least once, I might have been "accidentalized"—a popular phrase known to the victims, at the time—by another notorious top Special Branch official, after being lured away from a public function to "follow our car." I did, before I literally smelled death and drove out of the trap. Several times, I was trapped even by simple things, like protesting about the bust of Queen Victoria having overstayed its use in a once white-only club. Next to it was a portrait of Banda, the black president. The expectation was for me to transfer my feelings to him.

A committee comprised of the Malawi Congress Party, University, and police officials sat to decide my fate after I published "Chancellor College—a Personal View." I compared the college at the time I was one of the first students, in the mid-1960s, with the time when I was a lecturer, in the late-1980s. I was required to send copies of the article for vetting to the then-Principal of the college and the Vice-Chancellor. I was afterward invited to both offices to explain what had prompted me to write such an article and to remove certain observations I had made in my personal capacity.

Still, the truncated version was deemed offensive or subversive enough to warrant a special committee to convene. The secretary, who happened to be the Registrar, told me later, privately, that the unanswerable question was: didn't I know that the University of Malawi was a personal gift by His Excellency, the Life President, Dr H Kamuzu Banda? Fortunately, I was not invited to the meeting or it might have cost me my job and led to dire consequences, besides, if not my life.

An unexpected event in the mid-1970s was my finding a long-suppressed scholarship to study in the United States. So, I left a month earlier than everyone expected and spent it in England. I had, so I gathered later, beaten the dark forces, for the time being. Things had worsened when I got back in the early-1980s.

All the same, it is sometimes amazing, if not exasperating, to still be asked: how come you were not detained? Out of sheer exasperation, I changed my response to: how can you ask a survivor who's just swum across a crocodile-infested river, how come you were not eaten? In any case, victims were seldom told why they were being detained or thrown to be "meat for the crocodiles." Seldom did the carriers or the police know, either.

I can only give one of the readers' responses here: "'Napolo' is too complex to be understood, that's why you were not detained." "I hope so," I say ruefully. Over the years, as the "Banda days" passed but did not entirely recede, my poetry moved between the complex and the straightforward. I can see it myself, not as a matter of choice but theme, I guess. As the era eased, so did the poetry move to embrace day-to-day events. Even private citizens could tell you what they did to persons like you.

Rampant political hypocrisy, selective enrichment and programmed poverty, derailment of justice, crime with violence, disease and death, floundering of writers and artists: The poems in this volume reflect those stages in my life, from deliberate verbal camouflage to naked articulacy.

Some of the poetry has been labeled by critics "privatist," "personal," or using "private symbolism," and therefore difficult to understand. Writing under the watchful eyes of the Censorship Board, a wrathful regime, and a vengeful secret police, it was difficult to write "public" poetry, and get away with it. Even love poetry was scrutinized, open to dissection and likely to get the poet incarcerated. However, it was this very environment that was likely to produce the best poetry. Escaping into myth or history was more therapeutic than exploding into inarticulacy.

These then, are not really "collected" poems as such. I had to leave out some I thought would not be appropriate for this volume. Other "discards" belong to certain stages in my development of the craft of poetry. I hope you will enjoy what's here.

Napolo

I. Napolo

The Apocalypse

Mlauli's tomb roared:
"Mphirimo! Mphirimo! Mphirimo!
Kudzabwera Napolo!"
M'bona was checked in mid-leap,
Chilembwe turned over and went back to sleep.

Mulanje, Zomba, and Nyika fled their places,
whimpered and hid their faces.
Shire curled round its course and bit its tail.
Lilongwe reared its head but it was too frail.
Songwe exploded and threw its seed
into the lake where it caught typhoid.

Yes, it rained.
Oh, how it rained that time!
The parched throat of the earth drank it up,
swelled its stomach in pregnancy;
but it came so late,
and with it came Napolo.
Napolo gnawed the womb of the earth,
the earth groaned and aborted showing its teeth,
its teeth uprooted the trees on the banks,
the banks where birds sang around the python's flanks.

The Path

I washed my feet in the waters of Mulungusi
and anointed myself with the blood
of those Napolo had left unburied.
I tied the loincloth around me in a tight knot:
it was a perilous climb up Kaphirintiwa.

And did Napolo pass here indeed?
The trembling earth under my feet?
The roaring waters around my ears?
The hurtling mountains?

The desolation of the shrines
portends retribution
and revision.

And did Napolo pass here indeed?
Was all that for this?
This ritual of bloodletting?
And that to a deranged god creating
these strange forms of death?

I will to the mountain top
and there divine the message
Napolo brought.
I had washed my feet in the waters of Mulungusi.

The Messengers

Napolo has spoken: Death.
The lizard scuttled in the undergrowth;

the excitement he carried did not burden him.
Mankind awaited his coming.

Napolo has spoken: Life.
The Chameleon stopped to consider
a joint in his leg and hesitated.
He rolled an eye behind and in front,
the shrubbery swallowed his form.
Mankind awaited his coming.

Napolo has spoken:
The man in the loincloth came to us at dawn.
We gathered round to hear the message,
but did not understand.
He spoke to us in a strange tongue
and we greeted it with laughter.
He turned his back on us;
now we shall never know.
And yet Napolo had spoken.

The Message

Was it a decade after Napolo
I met you, friend?
No matter.
We lived to tell the story around the fire
in whispers and behind locked doors.
We are going to laugh together again
with empty mouths,
and dead eyes:
grimaces echoing hollowed minds.

Review what is left unsaid,
and, after we have parted,
we will know
what it is we wanted to say
before you noticed the dullness in my eyes
and I, the emptiness of your mouth,
before the art of saying nothing
in a mountain of words
interrupted our conversation.

In those days, my friend,
martyrs were left unburied,
heroes were coffined alive or fled.
Our tears remained unshed:
we did not know they had died.
No one told us who had gone.
These tears, my friend, are wrung
from a heart shattered
by the apocalypse
that was Napolo.

The Aftermath

Mlauli's tomb roared again:
"Mphirimo! Mphirimo! Mphiri-!"
The snarl of brakes strangled the sepulchral voice,
boots crunched the gravel,
and muzzles of machine guns
confronted the dawn.
Napolo was here
to stay.

II. Napolo Metamorphosis

The Metamorphosis

It glared at us in the dailies,
scorched the telephone wires,
was screamed over the radio,
we heard it from breathless mouths,
the whirlwind uprooted the rooftops,
to hurl it round our heads.
The metamorphosis of Napolo
needed no Mlauli's sepulchre
to announce the return.

The man in the loincloth also
discarded the trappings
of his profession.
Bark cloth was no longer
considered appropriate
and oracular voice too faint
to be heard above the tumult
of expectancy.
Field green replaced bark cloth,
the divining rod
thundered fire and smoke.
The nation held its breath:
there had been nothing like it before.
A lifetime of spiritual somnolence,
        intellectual malnutrition,
        improvised existence,

> pressurised underdevelopment,
> programmed exploitation,
needed Napolo to rouse it.

Napologia

The man advised: to see
the teeth of Napolo is patience;
wait until Napolo has gone
and ululate: I am blessed.
The youth answered:
the goat that delayed
got the lash on its behind;
when the sun shines
one knows Napolo has gone.
Then is the time to rejoice.

The man warned:
the weather is like genitals,
it suddenly changes—don't trust it.
The youth retorted:
when you have husbanded lightning
you do not quake at the flashes,
and he who cries for rain
cries for mud too—if not Napolo.

Son, a stranger does not beat the drum.
Father, the fool beat the drum while
the clever one danced.
—You know, two cocks do not crow
under the same roof.

—No, but a cock does not crow away from home.
The man exhorted:
the arrow that takes long in aiming
suddenly falls in the eye.
The youth replied:
the bird had perched right on the bow,
so we could not kill it.
Then the man admonished:
to punish a monkey
you do not arrow it:
smash its head.
The youth was silent.

The man concluded:
the old dog does not scratch in vain;
the words of the elders
are appreciated only
with the passage of Napolo;
the river Tinkanena
flows into Siizi.
But the youth had the last word:
old pepper is never hot;
tough luck for the old stalk,
the maize cob waits for
the fire—next time!

The Sons of Napolo

We danced the Ingoma
in worsted wool and crimplene,
shoes strapped to our jiggered soles.

The shields we carried
were emblazoned with a motto
written in a foreign tongue.
We danced Nyau steps
to the rhythm of rock 'n' roll:
sycophants to the frenzied music
of our adopted forefathers.

We put tithes
not into extortionate offertory baskets
but bottomless terylene pockets.
The sign of the cross
confused the clapping of hands;
the amens drowned
the ululation to our new gods.
Religiously paying homage
to the four wheels of a Benz;
worshipping images,
grimacing our passwords,
and our passports to survival
in the continual emasculation of existence.

We bared our teeth in complicity
with the daylight sacrilege,
and joined fervently
in the dehumanized chants
of the new dispensation,
under the chilling, pious eye
of the guardian of our traditions.

Moral elephantiasis
is infectious, my friend.
He who guards the well
does not die of thirst;
and if you can't beat 'em
join 'em.

III. Napolo: In the Beginning

Seeds cracked in the sultry afternoon,
the desiccated undergrowth sizzled,
stifling new life in its pods,
twigs snapped,
wilting trees panted in the long drought.

       *   *   *

Ambuye.
Pepa.
Akumasoka.
Pepa.
Akumizimu.
Pepa.

For seven nights
your sons have not known their wives.
Pepa.
For seven nights
your daughters have not seen the moon.
Pepa.
For seven nights
have we purified ourselves.
Pepa.

Listen, then, to the cries
of your sons and daughters.

Eyes downcast,
the virgin placed the basket of flour
beside the pot of beer and withdrew.
The *nsolo* tree rustled its leaves.
The man in the loincloth,
arms raised, listened.
                *   *   *

A yawn and gentle stirring,
Changula had opened his eyes.
Li Li Li
The blast bowed the trees,
genuflecting grass remained
on bended knees.
Phiti Phiti Phiti
Changula, forerunner of Napolo,
opened his mouth wide,
howled down the mountain slope,
spun the trees and grass on their heels
to rocking attention,
as the whirlwind,
writhing on its head,
stripped and assaulted
all in its path
and sped on.
                *   *   *

Stillness.

Then the air resounded
with thunder and lightning,
earth's mouth gaped wide.
Trees, boulders, villages,
were sucked into its entrails,
ground and ejected down river.
Heads, arms, legs, chests,
disemboweled earth churned
in the furious current.

The earth bled,
reeked of mud and mangled flesh,
guts bubbled in the torrent.
Gubudu Gubudu
Gubudu Gubudu
Zomba detonated its boulders
and blasted a pathway
down its slope.
Mulungusi was born:
Napolo had decreed it.

Beggar Woman

I

   And will the lice,
   having intimations of my death,
   flee from my body
   like rats abandoning a sinking ship
   or fleas a dying hedgehog?

I have felt my hair—that lush breeding ground—
stand on its toes to make hairways and highways
for flatulent bellies of overfed lice and unhatched eggs.
   The eggs hatch into little ones,
   the little lice grow into big ones,
   and they all suck my soul,
   play hide-and-suck on cloth and hair.

They have coursed the great forests of my hair,
created the well-beaten pathways of tiny feet,
clawing and gorging their way through the tufts.
   The black ones claim my head,
   the light-skinned ones my body.
   The glinting patches, the bloody splotches,
   the skeletons are all signs of their progress.

And alone at night I have recorded their work songs,
these humming wonderworkers draining my life-blood,
felt the caress of prowling feet and the love bites.
   The syncopation of hunting feet,
   the gush of blood from the unlucky,

23

another louse dead.
The explosion of a swatted louse:
die, louse, die.

Single-handed I have fought titanic battles in my rags,
nightly unleashed imprecations, fingers, and fingernails,
at vanguards, and horde after horde, of gigantic lice.
   Lean-bellied militants and revolutionaries,
   the riot squad and iron-jawed warriors,
   reading the Declaration of Lice Rights:
   the right to live on unclaimed territory.

And I have woken up in the mornings ululating,
counted my conquests like I count my daily takings
of genocidal nights from the folds of my cloth.
   I have peeled, scraped, and wiped off
   blotched carcasses, mangled corpses,
   raged at the giant blobs of blood,
   the smear of lice juice on black skin.

What they want from me, a withered beggar woman,
what they want from the shriveled dugs, I don't know,
surely they can find juicier conquests out there?
   On affluent streets, in carpeted offices,
   the teeming buses, the gutting planes,
   the Toyotas, the Benzes, the Royces,
   the Titanic, the Ilala, the Queen Elizabeth?

Surely there are more choice parts,
jeweled arms, powdered pits, breasts,

perfumed underwear and petticoats
to play games of hide-and-suck in?

Yielding bellies on sumptuous beds,
succulent bottoms on feathered mattresses,
shampooed hair in air-conditioned hotels,
are these not for you and yours too?

II

I can no longer count the sighs and tear-drops
on my bloodstained fingernails and *chirundu*,
nor can I weigh songs and laughter frozen in me
by the scars and fresh wounds of my ragged soul;
too much blood has flowed already to mingle
with myriad lies and dismembered hopes;
many lives have abandoned truckloads of promises.

> When the stomach cannot share
> the blood the heart has pumped,
> the stomach turns upon itself
> and feeds upon its own sweat.

I have wrested the beatitudes from the preacher's lips,
thunderbolted them into the teeth of the whirlwind,
and watched double-headed worms transmogrifying;
for I too, have been to the mountain-top in my *chirundu*,
have felt the rock of Kaphirintiwa on my bare feet;
for I too, have paid my dues at Msinja and Nsanje,
and have walked trunks of dreams under each arm.

I crouch here in a thicket of ashes,
forging words and lives,
forging the past and the future,
forging the present.

I retrieve from the embers scarred and charred ends
of napalm-coated words, fractured lives and pasts,
atomised futures and presents melting here and now.
I cool them with sighs and tears of brothers and sisters
and fling them, sizzling conundrums, exploding
or rebounding on the granite-faced rock of Kaphirintiwa,
but I hear only cremated echoes of radioactive skeletons.
Echoes of images salvaged
from disremembered shrines;
metaphors of other timeless forges
that weld our present and our future.

III

What the elders said is true:
when the rain sees your dirt,
especially with lice too,
it does not stop.
Yet she who has espoused lightning
does not fear the flashes.

I have seen many rains too:
Napolo found me in the streets.
I sought sanctuary in the shops,
the offices, the church, the school,
but they had all put up the sign:

'Trespassers Will Be Persecuted',
so I walked into the teeth of Napolo,
to a lonely and ancient *nsolo* tree;
I knelt, trembling, in the mud,
and washed my bloodstained *chirundu*;
naked, I squeezed lice between my fingers:
between fingernail and fingernail.
Blood, rain and tears washed over me
and ran in torrents downhill.
I cleansed the knotted corners of my soul,
clogged by lice and clusters of lice eggs;
I shook my hair loose and hurled off
soot, ashes, bats' droppings, and lice;
and my womb quickened with dirges.
I watched torsos of lizards, squashed mice,
entrails of chameleon and cockroach shells
eddying in the whirlpools around me.
And at every lightning flash I could see
the upturned faces of drowned varmints
in the gutters, the sewers, the streams,
swirling past the shops, offices, church doors.
Every lightning flash illuminated me
and the havoc my god had wreaked:
bloated snakes, scorpions, crows, vultures:
dismembered phantoms from Napolo's menagerie
frothing and surging in the furious vortex.
       In the aftermath of Napolo,
       I emerge from the chaosis
       and march down rainbathed pavements
       singing on the fingernails of the rainbow.

27

Obituary

He was a blessing one never prays for—
lightning coming uninvited
while men, women, and children flee
in terror at Mphambe's wrath;
but, once the god has struck
and buried his bolt in the earth,
they rush to the riven place,
claw at its charred remains,
if a tree, at its bark or splinters:
the closer to the thunderbolt,
the more potent the charm.

He was a gift one never utters thanks for—
locusts swarming after the planting rains
while men, women, and children watch
with desperate hearts and raging eyes,
their tender shoots ravished by a horde
of sharp teeth and clicking jaws;
but, once darkness has descended,
run to grab the drooping bodies
and bring home basketfuls of heaven-sent food
from the ravaged greenery after the guests
have laid waste the year's promise.

He stood among us, divine,
listening to our songs,
supervising the rain dances,

receiving our sacrifices
of bull, goat, or cock,
drinking to the dregs
prayers fermenting in beer.

We sang praise songs:
He alone fought the *chidangwaleza*
that haunted the ancestral shrine.
He alone drank the *chilope* from its veins.
He alone shaved Changula's scales.

He sang his own refrains:
I know what broke the elephant's tusks
at the foot of the *dzaye* fruit tree.
I know what shriveled the feathers
from the old pheasant's head.
He met Napolo head-on.

Four Ways of Dying

The celebrants chanted
to the reluctant martyrs-to-be:
We would have a blood sacrifice!

The Crab's response:
I crawl
in my shell sideways,
        backwards,
        forwards
Avoid
        direct action on public matters,
        confrontation,
        commitment;
Meander
        to confuse direction or purpose,
                meaning,
                sense;
Squat
        to balance the issues,
        weigh,
        consider.

The Chameleon's answer:
Until I have exhausted my wardrobe,
lost my dye to a transparent nothingness,
free of reflection, true to my image,
I'll match my colors with yours,

snake my tongue out to your fears,
bare my teeth to puncture your hopes,
tread warily past your nightmares,
curl my tail round your sanctuaries,
clasp my pincer legs on your veins,
to listen to your heart beat.

The Mole's descent:
Wormlike I build in the entrails of the earth,
fashion intricate passages and halls,
tunnel Utopias and underground Edens,
substitute surface with subterranean vision,
level upon level of meaning of existence,
as I sink downward in my labyrinth,
to die in a catacomb of my own making.

The Kalilombe's ascent:
The gestation and questioning are over,
I'm restless with impatient fetuses,
belly-full with a profusion of conundrums.
My pilgrimage takes me to the cradle,
the *nsolo* tree, the lie-in of man's hopes.
I grit my teeth, grab the slippery surface
and hoist myself up the nation's trunk.
On the topmost branch I have momentary
possession of eternity whirling in the chaosis,
with the deathsong floating from my lips,
I fling myself down on Kaphirintiwa rock
as multivarious forms of art and life

issue out from the convulsions
of the ruptured womb;
and thus I die.

Derailment: A Delirium

I

I made the pilgrimage again
to the mountain-top to divine
how Napolo parted the waters,
the granite, chunks of earth,
tree trunks, and the skies,
creating the cataclysms
in the mountain, the psyche, and hepatitis.

I drove past my grandmother,
skin stark black under the white dress,
owl glasses glinting in the sunlight,
as I tore past her, waving.
She waved back,
and I wept at ninety miles an hour
wondering: had she got hepatitis too?

On the mountain-top
I parked at the end of the queue,
self-consciously inching my way
to the life-giving waters.
Started and stopped,
knowing the blockage had infected
the blood system, arteries, veins.
Started and stopped,
being careful not to disturb
migrant viruses and zombies.

Started and stopped.
Read a book, smoked, stared around
to count how many zombies
had gone before me,
how many were coming,
starting and stopping,
behind me, praying
I'd get there before
the sacred waters dried up.
Started and stopped.

II

I wanted to talk to the other suppliants
swirling around me like amoebas and viruses,
to deliberate the issues concerning the liver,
the causes and effects of the invasion
and the blockage.

Faces:
maimers of my psyche.
Faces:
'These days I only go out with contractors.'
Faces:
'These girls are really decent
but I guess I'll never convince you.'

Snakes
who had abandoned sloughing
formed a corporation
and now make their own

wash 'n' wear fabrics.
Polecats
bought shares in industry
to increase the pollution explosion.
Crocodiles
swam upstream among the marshes
and launched a tears-by-the-gallon campaign.
Cultists,
infected by moral elephantiasis
(not hepatitis),
preached the brotherhood
of all zombies.

But queuing in a car
is not conducive
to contact and dialogue:
metal and glass walls
block communication and vision,
and all I meet are chromium-plated
forms swimming in exhaust fumes:
cabbage-lives wrapping timid centers,
peanut-in-pod existences,
eyes of zombies queuing
at the fountain of life.

III

Now indeed Leza has fled this land.
Only Mphambe reigns toying with man,
and Chiluwe, past master in subterfuge,

brings locusts to the table,
leaving the fields bare;
joy to the mouth,
grief to the soul;
peace to the stomach,
war to the mind.

I think as I start and stop:
Wasn't it you groveling
at the foot of the *nsolo* tree,
imploring Chauta to tell you
why Napolo had passed here?
Wasn't it you pouring
libations thrice to know
the meaning of the drought?

And should I not now
lift up the loincloth yet again
from the rafters and ascend the peak
to read from the granite-faced
rock of Kaphirintiwa
the meaning of hepatitis?

But Chiluwe had beaten me to the fountain,
he and his United Witches' Corporation
ganging on his side riding baskets,
hyenas' backs, owls' wings,
and the *nzulule*'s night battle cry.

I paused in my stride:
Had I come back to this?
Hepatitis?

Hepatitis,
that was my enemy
and I didn't know it.
Just think of it:
Hepatitis was not across the border
but right here,
in the liver, within.

I ignored Chiluwe
and proceeded
unafraid
to the life-giving waters.

IV

Napolo spoke to me
in the waters regenerating my car:
'What kind of hepatitis, son?'
'Premium, please,' I said trembling.
And I saw hordes of them,
layer upon layer,
amoebas and viruses
debating what to do
with your liver.
Premium or Regular?
Amoebic or Viral?

What is hepatitis?
An administrator
wondering what web to spin
and how far across the room
it should reach?

How do you get hepatitis?
From friends speaking so close
you can count how many drinks
they had last night?

How can you tell the difference?
The colour of their eyes,
the palms or the soles of their feet,
a certain discoloration of the nails
tells they are not pedigree.

(And at night
I see your outline in the doorway;
see through to the liver blockage,
the bile flowing into the bloodstream
like petrol into my car.

Could you move
more centrally in the doorway
so I can see what you've got?
A or B Type?

You passed the doorway again,

three times in one morning,
wearing hepatitis.
I asked at last, innocent-like,
Each time you pass by
you have a different kind.
What kind is it this time?
Viral or Amoebic?
Premium or Regular?')

And I sat by the phone,
getting messages from satellites,
wondering at the same time:
Do satellites transmit hepatitis?
Operator, urgent, please,
I've got to talk to hepatitis.

V

At the fountain-head I stopped and prayed:
Chauta, I want my kids, the nanny, her kid and sister,
the sixty-year-old man we call garden-boy,
all inoculated against hepatitis,
so their livers don't get blockages,
their biles don't flood the bloodstream,
so their conjunctivitis doesn't mix with their colds,
their diarrhea, pinworm, and their arithmetic;
so they can sing the national anthem
in the garden as they play house;
so it doesn't interfere with their appetite
as they gather it, running, dancing, and riding
the only bike, it seems, in the neighborhood;

so it doesn't pass on to the CCAP kids
who, after school, politely enough,
walk to the front door, in spite of the puppy:
Could they please pluck off a few guavas
from the garden, they were hungry?
They are always hungry
since in the morning they visited
the tree without asking me.

Chauta, remember also, I told the kids
they could eat the guavas,
but to be careful with the hepatitis
flowering in the branches on the northern side.
It's infectious: Up to six weeks for the incubation,
up to six months in bed.
No guavas, no school, no dancing, no anthem,
only hepatitis.

Remember, too, watching them go to the tree,
swarming in the branches, even the northern ones,
I wondered how long it would take
to reach their livers.

VI

And she came to me floating upon the waters,
limpid in her *chitenje* like an after-swim
spirit-maid of Mulungusi, among the amoebas,
swirling in the chaosis with the viruses.

Napolo spoke to me again above the roar:
'It's the friendly kind,' he said.
He'd give me some nice things
to think about instead of nightmares;
give me some nice things to do, too,
like letting me finger her liver,
trace the bile oozing its way up the arteries,
to see how far it had got.
Like letting me share her hepatitis,
for better or for worse.
And that's being nice, really.
When she comes home again
we can go for a second honeymoon
to a hepatitis-free cottage
by the lake.

She spoke to me through the fumes:
'It's no mystery at all, really,
only a blockage of the liver,
a fortuitous derailment of the bile
outside the borders of gamma globulin;
the blockage playing havoc with the arteries
that feed the nation; an influx of amoebas and viruses;
something to be laughed away at cocktail parties;
a parliament of amoebas and viruses
assembling in the hostels of our being,
sorting out our livers, rifling our bile,
to see how far we can survive amoeba rights
to live in our liver.

Parasites.
Viruses.'

She ended her message with the usual:
'See you soon, I hope.'
As in the old song, I said:
'In a while, hepatitis.'

Three Songs

Tell me how a spirit dies.
Do worms claw at its flesh?
Spiders maul the skeleton?
And mold grow out of the heap?

The Wandering Spirit

The spirit in sojourn strains in its sanctuary,
musing at the voices riding the crest of the whirlwind.
Go, child, they whisper, but do not linger at the crossroads
when darkness is unsheathed to slay the sun's rays
and the jackal leaves his lair to howl in the wake.

But how was I to know the spirits also walked abroad
when the stars flickered and masked their faces
at the sound of the solitary caller's steps in darkness?
And I, too, clothed in the silken coat of darkness?

I gazed into the eddies of darkness wearing webs of silence
as the waves of night wound a cocoon round my soul
and the sinews of sorrow stretched before me to brood
against the support darkness had wrought and bred.
                    Does darkness wear mantles of happiness, too,
                    which, unbuttoned, reveal wreathes of smiles
                    meeting fellow spirits in the whirlwind?

Yet I would rip these walls,
rend the shrouds to shreds
and leap into the chaosis.

What god, tell me,
would say LET NOT MEN DIE
and give the message to the chameleon?

What god, tell me,
would say LET MEN DIE
and give the message to the lizard?

What man, tell me,
would receive one and reject the other?
What man could cling to both?

Yet I have seen the way strewn with corpses by the roadside;
joy and friendship mangled, abandoned to rot in the bushes;
tortured spirits and broken skeletons weeping in the wind:
arrow points of anguish and clubs of malice hardening the heart
till tumors of fear burst searing notches of dread in the soul.

The Dead

Straining against the shrouds smothering us;
breaking the ropes and mats mooring us;
scattering worms and mold from our rotting flesh;
rupturing mounds and walking the same way
we took when leaving mankind for our resting places,

we march by the shafts of early morning,
piercing the horizon to mingle with the living,
one hand holding man's lump of guilt in a potsherd,
the other carrying branches to fend off flies from the burden.
But what music meets the membrane of our return?
>
> You with the potsherds:
> vanish from our sight,
> your home is the grave.
> Why did you come back?

It is true we died long ago and they buried us.
Alongside our lives they laid also their memory and guilt;
but we had hoped at this hour, this time of reunion,
we would unload our burden and dance, glad of the relief.
Yet their fingers point at us and the song rings in our ears:
>
> You, Mangadzi, and you, Mbona,
> return to your graves.
> When we swept the dancing site,
> we were not singing your names.

We walk back the same way: the only funeral songs
our own anguish, faltering footsteps and buzzing flies;
back to the *nkhadzi* trees burdened with humiliation
at least the earth will not reject us in revulsion,
nor the worms and spiders we abandoned in our coffins.

Come, mold, sprout on the worms breeding under the shrouds
and the spiders weaving knotworks in the wood;
muzzle our mouths forever and let only the jackal howl here.

Come, rot, still our skeletons weeping to the winds overhead;
bury us deeper in our graves and stand guard over the mounds.

The Living

Emerging from the murky depths of Maravi pool at noontime,
after drinking the dregs of yesteryear's draught,
I saw Mphambe riding the barbed arrows of lightning,
his flashing eyes beating jagged flame-ways in the firmament,
and each stride scorching the earth beneath him to cinders.

Listening to the lament of the living in the embrace of woe,
I heard the strain smothering the tattoo of the sacred drum.
I did not think after this Mbiriwiri would send more oracles.
Indeed the drum that weeps loudest is soonest burst.
Had I not heard the moaning of the skin at the seams?

Oh, how scarlet-stained the sacred forests of Msinja!
The toilet at Mandevu's grocery-and-bar was knee-deep.
In the aftermath of Mphambe's thunder there was silence,
yet in the silence I saw words sprouting on spearheads
and dancing to the rhythm of demented wardrums.

> Words:
> tell me what we did in the year of the locusts.
> I can't remember.
> Don't you remember Napolo?
> What is Napolo?

Words:
Promise you won't tell my husband.
Of course not. How could I?
Njala, bwana, tandipatseni
wani tambala yokha, pulizi.

Words:
the shrine at Msinja has no verandah or eaves;
how can I seek refuge even in the shadows
of the granite-faced imprints of Kaphirintiwa?
So lend me a hoe to dig myself a sanctuary.

I heard the python crowing at the rainbow's earthing,
and saw him painting the archway red, yellow, and blue,
and I wondered how a spirit dies: Do worms claw at its flesh,
spiders maul the skeleton, and mold grow out of the heap?
The voices whispering in the whirlwind scorn mortality.

Of Promises and Prophecy

Prologue

Tomorrows reactivate somnolence,
todays perpetuate inertia
yesterdays diffuse dismembered hopes:
the eternal miasma of zombies,

smeared in disco lights,
lacerated with reggae sounds,
groping in the darkness between
the tavern, bar and rest house:

progress punctuated by puddles
of vomit, sweat, beer and wine,
the whore's smile and the thug's
demand for a light or else.

I

No, they shall not have the truth
for facts are explosives
in anonymous brown bags,
exploding between the fingers,
blowing reality into oblivion.

Let the few remaining honest souls
still roaming dangerously abroad
be lured again into the folds
of festering falsehood.

Let common knowledge become
the property of the minority
and mystification be manna
and hyssop for the masses.

And so, after taking some
for one or two rides
let us recede into the citadels
of silence and feed the people
with more lines of lies.

And under the shroud of silence
let retrospection unroll the map,
trace the tracks of introspection
to pinpoint where the derailment
and mass burial of truth took place.

II

No, don't jog memory any more,
let it coil as harmless
as a puff adder until it's stepped upon;
only add more fuel to the amnesia,
programmed inertia and somnolence.

Let the few tumescent egos still around
mass-produce psychic onanism,
pack them into portable and compact
shapes that will fit into trunks, cases,
bags, pocket books, and passports
saleable at the next port of entry.

Educate the masses with new tools
of ideological bio-feedback;
irrigate their drought-stricken spirits with
technological fried-while-you-starve,
computerized mind-swopping, malaise,
anomy, and emotional dehydration.

Arm the beggars, vagrants, peasants
with transistorized pleas, canned laughter;
mesmerize the workers with videotaped leisure,
press-gang local witches into astronauts,
cauterize hope, desire, and memory.

Where are the great plans now?
Where the blueprints?
What is the programme?
What now?

Epilogue

Shall I destroy the citadel
and rebuild it in three days?
Three days in which will rise
a monolith of groans, gasps, and gashes
that are mouths screaming silent,
soul-searing, razor-sharp agony?

Three days in which will sprout
a luxurious green gold garden

with patches of Marinas, Mazdas,
Fiats, Fords, Buicks, and Benzes?

Armed with a multi-pronged plan
Man-Against-Self-and-Society (MASS)
I descended from the mountain-top
with a blueprint of self-raising ideology,
improved-me conditions,
modern methods of mass-hypnosis,
and broke the citadels of silence.

Chingwe's Hole Revisited

I

Move your feet a little, dear rock,
as I squat in your shade.
Let me touch your petrified roots
in the aftermath of Napolo,
and gaze at chaosis in Chingwe's hole.
I reach out and the rock shrinks back,
quaking mimosa-like,
only to unfurl itself again
when I'm my shadow's length away.

Like a medicine-man in the moonlight,
hunting for a virulent root
hidden under the scaly claws
of Changula on the craggy face
of the mountain, I wore amulets
and notched tattoos
in the interfaces of memory
as a preamble to my peregrinations.

I moved among the débris, sherds, and bones,
poked fingers into the myth-infested crevices,
cocked an ear to the bird song in a *nsolo* tree
on the banks of a pool nearby.
(They say the chemical composition of the redness
in the water is no longer a mystery,
considering oxidation, and all that.)

What do I seek in this ancient place?
Chiluwe, the mystifier? Changula?
Images in a potsherd?
Cremated echoes of radioactive myth?
What do I want from this brainchild
of tired tourists?

(This poem should be written on one hundred percent recycled
paper.
It is only recycled myth written by a recycled poet twice removed.)

II

I sat by the edge of Chingwe's Hole,
listening to the truncated refrains
hovering uncertainly in the crannies.
Chameleon-eyed, I surveyed the streams
drained from their sources,
laying bare silt, roots, boulders,
and channels of mystification.

(When contradictions unravel the strands
of lies we have so carefully knit,
when webs of silence wear so thin
migrant spiders abandon their flies,
chameleons also lose their dye:
you can see their innards.)

How tiny the rock of Kaphirintiwa looks now
from the edge of the plateau!

It hadn't seemed that small
even from the top floor of Delamere House.

(We must move the unformed rock, they said,
to another place;
before the afforestation, you know. Detonations.
Just imagine a thousand pieces of exploded ore
        and lore
                floating
                        whirling
                                eddying
                                        down the slopes
enough to make professors, urchins, street vendors
sneeze in the valley below.
Indeed, I was caught in the fallout too.
Perhaps when the dust settles, I will mark the spot:
The rock of Kaphirintiwa landed here.
Under whose hands was the rock moved, you ask?)

Itinerant *kalilombe*s are rare these days;
their parturition songs sound faint too,
especially so far away from home,
computing their kwacha, lives, and hopes,
programming their virtues to show their young
how it was before I moved the rock, myself.

(Sometimes I wake up at night terrorized by a question:
Is schizophrenia hereditary?
Will it pass on to my children like genes, et cetera?)

III

History covered Chingwe's Hole
with fungal inspiration
delivered in packages labeled:
psychoses ready-made;
traumas made-to-measure;
paid for as an intellectual piece
of ritual protection
against the perception of reality.

The truth lay in the abyss of the hole,
plummeted over the precipice,
     bounced against
          the outgrowths,
               reverberating
in the jagged psyche.

Chingwe's Hole assaulted me
out of the lethargy of apathy;
paralyzed me with probes
in the crevices of the mind;
flagellated the prostrate self
to a nightmarish mass of bio-feedback
anticipating the ultimate.

I tossed in the chaosis of the whirlwind,
sped on, whirling, a particle in an electronic nightmare,
pursued by zombies riding the phosphorescent backs
of the city lights below.

I got concussion at the crossroads,
short-circuited by a wayward current
(Press Button B To Reactivate)
plugged to the centri- or the petrifugal
forces of someone else's dream.

The zombies prised me open,
parting the strands of my own dream,
draining out globules of images,
dislodging rooted recollections,
and displayed them:
one phantasm to another.

I writhed and gyrated, a displaced fetus
holding fast to the chaosis
on the back of the whirlwind.

(Rock, please, let me hold your knee.
I don't want to die, yet.)

IV

I was lured to the shade of the rock
by Chiluwe's arts and lullabies;
Chiluwe, performing frenetic dances on the rock,
waiting for Napolo to surface from the womb of the earth.

When Napolo bent an elbow,
placed stony fingers on the stubble of his chin;
and when the valley hoisted her flanks

to meet the craggy gaze of the prodigal above,
yearning for another visit to the shimmering waters
of the lake below;

The three thousand feet of sinuous thrill
tilted on unbalanced shoulders
      renting shrouds,
          rupturing wombs,
              razing shrines,
                    raking wounds,
as the cataclysm
ground his subterranean peregrinations
in the convulsions of Mulungusi
to sojourn in the ripples of the lake.

And when Napolo, eternal, bloodied,
ancient chaosis
after the complicity and the complacency,
emerges from the oblivious waters,
what revisitation? What devastation?

And when my grandmother, that perpetual watcher,
(Napolo is going to return, son.)
hears Napolo's scales detonating the boulders
on his way back to the womb of the nation,
whose startled limbs will hurtle
into the chaosis that was Chingwe's Hole?
What will petrify Napolo in his hole forever?

(Napolo's itinerary remains incomplete, you see.
So does my poem. Hence the recycling.
Chiluwe, mischief-maker, still dances on the rock
sending his shadow into *Napolo's Hole*.)

A Death Song

(Birimankhwe maso adatupa ninji?
Kwathu maliro.
m'samaseke ana inu:
kwayera mbee, mbee, mbee.

Ine n'dzachoka pam'dzi pano;
mutsale mumange pam'dzi pano.
Taonani pakhomo pangapa:
payera mbee, mbee, mbee.)

I

(Chameleon, why are your eyes swollen?
There's death at home.)

The Chameleon was wrong.
The tear-stricken swollen
swiveling eyes did not see
the lizard still scuttling
on the potsherds of Kaphirintiwa;
did not hear the Kalilombe's
survival song as she burst open
to give birth to laughter, song, and dance.

Yes, the locusts came
and joined the army worms
and the monkeys in the middle

of the maize, bean, and groundnut gardens;
but the west brought AIDS
and hybrid maize to replenish
the ravished sturdy local stock.
The east brought yaws too,
in nice neat rice packets,
and the media promised us
another bumper harvest because
of the prevailing peace and prosperity.

II

>   (Look at my homestead:
>   it's empty, empty, empty.)

The Chameleon was wrong.
The homestead was not really empty.
Some zombies were left,
in spite of their deafness.
The *ndondocha*s wailed at night
despite their tongues being cut off.
They were not yet completely dead.

Yes, carloads of souls
met their sticky ends
at the end of the line.
However, the survivors were permitted
to attend the funerals and burials
under careful supervision.

III

(I shall leave this village;
you stay behind and build this village.)

The Chameleon was wrong.
The answer was not to abandon the village
as rats do a sinking ship
or fleas a dying hedgehog.
Exile, pretended, genuine,
or self-imposed, is not the answer
to the holocaust or the apocalypse.

Yes, we seek new homes every day,
the old ones no longer habitable.
We hunt for new myths everywhere,
the ancient ones defaced or defiled.
However, recycled myths or homes
are better than nothing,
they are all we have left.

IV

(Do not laugh, children:
it's empty, empty, empty.)

You are wrong, Chameleon.
Just look at the survivors:
How many Nyanjas did not hurtle
headlong into Chingwe's Hole?
How many Ngonis did not
partake of the *kalongonda*?

How many Chewas were not
crushed at Mpata-wa-Milonde?
How many Kafulas did not
suffocate in the Bunda caves?

Yes, you are wrong, Chameleon.
Just count how many delayed
their deaths in spite of the lizard's message.
Look how laughter, song, and dance
still rebound against the rock
of Kaphirintiwa:
We are still alive!

Writers' Workshop Revisited

Perturbation sat on my scraping chair
as I stared at contours of commitment
or furrowed faces puzzling over a line.
It climbed up to the membrane of my memory
and switched on shots of other backs
and brows captured in similar stances.

Shall I say, there sat *Nkhumbutera*,
a packetful of poetry in his pouch?
He wrote and left, but came back
and sat between the sheets of a double bind.
They had convinced him totally
there was no sustenance anywhere else,
even in his own homestead of old.
Now he lives on the split lines of reality.
There perched little *Chelule*, precariously
dozing but not dropping off entirely.
The elevated discussion flapped around him.
He was content to be counted, among chameleons.
Only he finally went into a long sleep:
the pocketful of poems are now ant-ridden,
a cryptic rubble punctuated by earth,
scraps and his rotting feathers.

You couldn't touch *Nunkhadala*,
not for ritualistic reasons anyway,
but for the guardian flies he bred.

He trapped them in his verses, too,
after luring them on with a brilliant image,
a melodious line and promises of publication.
They buzzed too close and he escorted them
to their doom in a covered car or wagon.

Kadzioche posed as priest of poetry,
daring images, allusions and innuendos.
He fluttered forth on stormy nights,
between the frying pan and the fire.
He flew too near the flames one time
and sustained multiple burns of his own choice.
He curled round his own stinking corpse,
singed wings and seared hair.

Kafadala, the late bloomer,
should not have gone, really.
Him and his transparent verses.
Everyone knew what he was talking about.
He had not the art of the chameleons.
He went in but came out and stayed out.
Now not even echoes of his songs
reach us back here to the survivors.

The real *Kalilombe* enfolded us fondly;
a pincer leg pinioning a blooming image;
one eye swiveling at a wayward word,
the other pointing to a promising metaphor;
a tongue snaking out at tortuous lines,

a tail curled round prizewinning verse;
and at each session, before our eyes,
she hatched a new kind of chameleon.

Shall I say, I have sat here before
with warm visions and reflections,
heard echoes from Ibadan and beyond,
while waiting for the glorious sunset
to come to the heights of Sapitwa?
Lord, let your servant depart in peace
after having heard your first *mau*,
witnessed Napolo in the aftermath
of incarcerated chameleons and gods
till my exiled brothers come home,
or else we shall all become nightwatchers
in our nightsongs, singing to our hearths.

Chameleon-eyed I surfaced to the present
and surveyed the familiar scene and signs,
and wept, not for the past chameleons
but the *ndondocha*, tongueless, doomed
to mouthings and wailings to clogged ears.
I shed *nkhadzi* tears at *msendawana*,
gone in stillbirths of aborted arts
and artists never to see the light.

But as the night shadows fought nostalgia
with our present terrors, you and I knew
that the old chameleons were not yet dead,

completely gone, or silenced, forever;
that the ancient *kalilombe* was with us still,
and will be the last to go with her death song.

Lies Unlimited

Napolo unraveled again
the stitches of lies
we had so carefully sewn
in the seams of empty rhetoric.
Ours was a patched-up job,
like a beggar's rags
with the strands showing
how our words forked out,
covering stillbirths of truths,
dismemberment of accuracy.
Each patch confronted
a manufactory of lies:
the different ideologies
and looms it had lived through.

In our anecdotage
we replayed the disasters
we had erected as monuments
inherited by a reluctant posterity.
Contradictory fabrications
like those of a chameleon
partly camouflaged as he fleets past
flowers, greenery and promontories.
The replays at the *bwalo*,
palavers, and meetings,
rallies and conventions

forced us into a profound vacuity
as the clichés of circumlocution,
diversions, deviations and distortions
rebounded on mere verbiage.

Lies, coming out in two pitches
like the hooting of an owl:
the first one for listeners,
loud and triumphant;
the second one for us,
muted and anguished.

Truth lived on precariously
refusing to be stitched
together in the interfaces
but darting out dangerously
like the tongue of the *kalilombe*
lashing and spitting out words,
long-reaching and prophetic.

There was no revolution, really:
that was a grand mystification.
We manufactured instant heroes:
our martyrs were *msendawana*,
the *kadzioche* and the *kafadala*
enriching sycophantic warriors
parading their unglorious battles
and entries into a collective amnesia.

Now only professional mourners,
with piri-piri tears flowing hotly,
do the rounds daily, dirging
to our own wakes, lamenting
like inarticulate *ndondocha* to
lay bougainvillea wreathes
in the village graveyards,
as planeloads and truckloads
ululate as they dance past us,
replaying the old subterfuges:
hypnotic as the *chelule* chant
making us soporific still,
fascinated by the enchanter;
blatant as the *nkhumbutera* song,
making us believe for safety
we really have to fall in line,
for there is no sustenance
even in our own homesteads.
Only Napolo revealed the lies.

Meanwhile in the Drought

I

There are no more corpses nor cadavers here,
strewn on the sizzling roadsides or bare lands,
no vultures nor hyenas circle in the drought,
nor crows, nor flies in the rubbish pits.

The skeletons, like blood relations, dare not
rot but, being too dry already, ignite in
spontaneous combustion, enkindling long
forgotten jealousies, malices and frictions.

The crops in the fields desiccate leisurely
while standing on their dehydrated stalks.
The mice flee from the roasting gardens
to join the rats in the empty granaries and eaves.

The hollowed moos of emaciated cows mingle
with the grunts of pigs at dry water-holes.
The cockroaches compete with the weevils
to gnaw at the last grain in the baskets.

II

Aid came at last to the refugee camps,
only it stayed there and did not reach us.
And how to be a refugee in your own land
became the only passport to the survival game.

So we changed our names and even nationalities,
moved our households and even our relations,
lost our conscience to resettle in the next camp,
where solace came from beyond the seas.

We camped, decamped and recamped again
to new sites like any other refugee rat,
migrating according to the seasonal aid
and changes in the international climate.

The national conscience was also emptied,
drained, washed clean, and overturned
like a beer pot, to dry in the scorching sun,
so eloquent, audible and visible to all.

Moral elephantiasis wound its way round
the ventricles of the moribund policy-makers,
but it too was beaten like a flour basket
to empty it of any remaining granules.

Only vacuous vaults, containers and receptacles
proclaim loudly the moral myopia infecting
commissions of enquiry, assessors, estimators
investigating how many were still surviving.

Donations, aid programs and other packages
besieged us daily in briefcases and trunks,
suits and overcoats, via the lake resorts,
motels and hotels, to invade us in boardrooms.

We surrendered our pride, arms waving aloft,
pleading for a truce, a détente or consultation;
dismantling all trappings of independence,
burying a checkered history of self-sufficiency

And yet Napolo had passed here several times.
The deluge floated our homes, cows and cars
from the mountain slopes down to the lake.
It spared not man, goat, granary nor tree.

But now Chingwe's Hole gapes to the dry skies,
empty of any statements, meaning or explanation.
No more downpours came to unleash Napolo.
The chameleons and the *kalilombe* are silenced.

How can the *kalilombe* sing new songs now,
for they know even if the deluge came again
it would be too late to save this year's crop
which was supposed to stave off last year's famine.

Meawhile the last *ndondocha* was slaughtered.
Even the *msendawana* was brought to table.
Squeamish witches and reluctant wizards
feasted, but it was not for a rain sacrifice.

Developments from the Grave

I

We have come full circle,
it seems: burying our dead
right in the homestead now,
on the sites the living had built.

We no longer bury our corpses
over there and away from us,
overhung by weeping *nkhadzi* trees
just as the missionaries advised us.

We have come full circle,
at last: burying our dead
deep in the soil beneath us;
we climb over the mounds daily.

We no longer hang the cadavers
high in the trees away from scavengers:
hyenas, ants, beaks and talons;
just as the colonials instructed us.

II

We brought the dead to the homestead,
revived them as *ndondocha*,
cut off their tongues and tamed them
to live in our granaries forever.

Bumper harvests come out of them
and we know who keeps the most,
organizing them into one task force
to labor in the tobacco, tea and cotton estates.

We unearthed the youth for *msendawana*
to skin them for their precious leather
and made purses out of the tender skin
for the most potent charm of them all.

We know who has the largest purse
accumulating wealth, and more.
Out of the mounds of our youth
sprout palaces, fleets and monuments.

III

Development did not catch us
by surprise, asleep or unprepared:
We knew about space exploration;
we had our own flying baskets.

The greenhouse effect is not news;
we know how to heat or cool the land:
Drought comes from a society on heat;
rain comes from a cooled nation.

But development came from the graves,
too full and closely packed to grow any more.
The protective *nkhadzi* trees fenced
each effort to force the grave boundaries.

We have now come full circle,
rightly so: living with our dead,
not only in *nsupa* or spirit houses
but in granaries, purses and coffins.

The Sinking Cenotaph

I

Your cenotaph sinks in the soaking soil.
Soon the concrete will crack the coffin,
splitting the woodwork in splinters,
and your corpse disintegrate in the depths.

Your sinking cenotaph disappears from the surface.
Soon it will cease to be a beacon on the horizon.
As the rotting leaves, grass and mud reclaim the land,
no one will realize there was once a cenotaph here.

Your chilling policies came to a dead end
as soon you became frigid in rigor mortis,
and their memory will likewise be smothered
as the monumental cenotaph sinks under.

Your four cornerstones no longer sustainable,
the epitaph on the cenotaph not your own,
soon they too will disappear with the edifice:
no one will recollect your pronouncements.

II

When we compute how many centimeters
the cenotaph sinks each rainy season
dread fills the empty spaces around it
as we also count those gone on your account.

The insects gnawing through the woodwork
can never forget our own lost relatives.
The worms wriggling in your rotting flesh
are fresh reminders of our own lost chances.

When they carried your coffin to hero's acre
we wept for journeys to our own graveyards.
When they lowered you to these grounds.
we lamented over the premature demises.

When they wept crocodile tears over you
we remembered real crocs in the Shire
which shed theirs as they gobbled ours,
thrown into the river by your minions.

III

There was the family across the border,
whose remains splattered over the room,
from a petrol bomb wrapped up as a gift.
A dissident's exile was no longer protection.

There was the death-ride of other subversives,
packed in a small saloon presumed on the run.
They collided head on with a wayward tree.
No evidence was forthcoming on how they died.

There were the truckloads of sycophants
who perished on the highways and waterways.
No obituaries mourned their demise in the papers.
Their screams strangled songs of loyal stalwarts.

There was this wrapper of words in metaphors
condemned to oblivion; there was the carver
of stone into art; singer, actor, dancer
all incarcerated for not composing your panegyrics.

IV

Sighing over sinking cenotaphs thinking
they will rise again to full stature
is a futile exercise of shallow minds:
cenotaphs are built over yawning holes.

*In memoriam*s should not be engraved on cenotaphs
sinking slowly under their guilt-laden weights.
Each brick tells the story of a victim beaten to death,
the concrete and mortar the tale of tortured flesh.

Now each dead victim heeds the rallying call.
His or her spirit heads for the cenotaph.
The spirits of the victims vie for a perch,
complete for a place with owl and *mzulule*.

It is not the dead weight of the coffin,
the concrete, brick, and mortar on top;
neither the rains nor the soft earth are doing it:
It is the sojourning spirit sinking the cenotaph.

The Road to Thakadzo

I

The concrete column supine on the road
Ambushes our cruising, overloaded car.
My wife, sons, and daughter exhale breaths
At one hundred and ten kilometers an hour
Past constricted throats killing spontaneous screams.

This is the aftermath of our family celebration
In Blantyre, to make it more memorable.
It would have been immemorable, even beyond,
Had the road block not seemed so insurmountable,
Undemocratic, and the brakes not functioned.

The heartstrings strained in their moorings
As the skid still took the car through.
The sumptuous dinner gestating in the stomach
Threatened to find its own reverse route
To splatter and rain on the tarmac road.

Was this crumpled column specially for us?
An articulated truck had just grunted past us
In the opposite direction: no signs of concrete
On its snout: it could not have flown over the ambuscade,
Sprawling like a snake after a feast on mice.

The escape route was a tiny strip by the side.
Beyond it beckoned the darkness and death,
Hiding, waiting with pangas, clubs, and guns,
To disembowel us and disgorge the family dinner
As the thugs finished us off, if we had not swerved.

II

The night on the road to Mangochi was similar:
Rocks and boulders across the highway of life;
Yelling thugs in the dim periphery of our lights;
Primitive chants dancing for our chilled blood.
We had been celebrating another year of survival.

The escape route was not different, either:
A tiny strip of space for a small car to squeeze;
A heave of relief as we passed the ambuscade;
A choked chorus from the family all around,
As adrenaline accelerated on tar at 110 kph.

Trembling breaths exhaled: saved again,
From the crumpled metal on bolders and rocks;
Hefty hacks from several sharpened pangas,
Finishing strokes or clubs in earnest hands,
From maniacal thugs single-minded on the mission.

What if the escape route was not there?
Which thug had masterminded this poor handiwork?
Had we come upon them prematurely?
And when they saw our tail lights escaping
Did they curse: another mission unaccomplished?

III

The night on the Thakadzo road was similar, too:
Metaphors concussed on the footprints of creation,
Ambushed by Philistines dancing on inspiration,
Goaded on by Chiluwe, the mystifier.
I was on another pilgrimage to Kaphirintiwa.

The escape route was not different, either:
A finger of light for poetry to pierce through;
A shuddering of the spirit as I surmounted again
Another writer's nightmare, another artist's ambush,
As a torrent of verbal imagery ejaculated forth.

Quivering spasms of poetic rebirth: saved again
From oppressive predators and intellectual cadavers,
Abortive attempts from unfettered mediocrity,
Obliterating unshackled thoughts, their time come,
Escaping from verbal detention by a derailed democracy.

What if the escape route was not there?
Which Philistines had done this inept work?
Had I vanquished the mercenaries of creativity?
And when they view another fiasco of their act
Will they pronounce: ambush the Mlakatuli?

IV

Memory took another route in history,
Of Mbona leaping from peak to peak,
Fleeing from his machinating enemies.

He had no car, then, to be ambushed,
Yet he met his fate in Nkhulubvi forest.

John Chilembwe, more recent history,
You can almost smell his spilled blood
As his road to destiny met another ambush.
He had no car, then, or even bicycle,
Yet he confronted his martyrdom bravely.

Dunduzu Chisiza had a car: a death trap.
Assailants don't read *Africa: What Lies Ahead*;
They only read what lies on the Zomba road.
He had more vision then, than, his enemies,
Yet Malawi, what lies ahead is now aborted.

Sangala, Gadama, Matenje, Chiwanga,
Visionaries crammed in one Government Minister's car,
Each separate dream dismembered ruthlessly.
The road to Mwanza has its own tale to tell,
Yet they had their plans squashed on tar.

Was it like this when the Vipya floundered?
Was it like this, too, when truckloads sank
At Liwonde to be meat for political crocodiles?
Or chartered planes crashed without reason?
The engineers were efficient: the victims died.

Past Hero-Bearing Age

I. The Repatriation

These bones need no amnesty
declared as for our exiled politicians
in the new, democratic Second Republic,
but, like our own artworks gracing
galleries and museums in foreign lands,
need to be brought expediently home
with all the media noise we can muster
and all the political fanfare possible.

These bones need no import-duty-paid
computed on their landing at Customs,
like computers, videos, fridges, or cars.
No, they are not even of foreign manufacture.
True, they exported themselves to exotic lands,
as we do our coffee, cotton, and tobacco,
but really they are still local produce,
coming home to be buried in the heroes' acre.

These bones have now acquired new labels:
martyrs, heroes, founders of the new democracy.
These are the real fighters of the Second Republic.
(How public and political temperaments change!)
True, when they fled then, so unceremoniously,
the political rhetoric branded them differently:
as rebels, dissidents, opposition ingrates,
but that was in the dark era of despotism.

II. The Bones' Tales

Let us turn the bones over again.
Let us sift the mold covering them.
Let us retrieve only the hidden heroism,
lest it rot with the dust and mold.
We have nothing to show posterity.
except for these repatriated bones.
which each have their own tale to tell.

These bones of the fearless journalist
met a sudden and violent end.
Imagine the explosion hurtling in
through the unsuspecting open window,
blowing the occupants to smithereens.
It is only the merciful eyes of Chauta
that could tell the intimate pieces apart.

Now we can have at least eight coffins.
In the land of the dead, there is democracy.
They say, too: one corpse, one coffin,
however intimately the loving pieces
were mixed with the debris afterwards,
or even however far the flesh and bones
were flung round the innocent house.

The bones of this old politician
also experienced an unnatural demise.
They euphemistically explained
that he had eaten some prison food

that had disagreed with him.
They laid him in the prison cemetery.
He too deserves his lot in the heroes' acre.

These bones of the young politician
died in controversial circumstances,
as our noisemakers render it.
An aura of mystery, terror, and horror
halos them, shrouding the coffin.
He led a revolutionary army of compatriots.
His whole village was wiped out.

These, and a lot more, are not new bones.
They belong to the old era of terror,
that of death and darkness, as one put it.
They cannot engender the aged soil,
when the land cries for a new era of heroes
and the Earth Mother pleads menopause.
She is, she says, beyond hero-bearing age!

III. The Heroes' Acre

Just as well we're repatriating them now.
Just imagine the pilgrimages of relatives,
friends, and sycophants to pay homage
to bones in cemeteries in foreign lands.
At what cost and with how much grief?

Now the bones are just a bus-ride away.
We can visit them every other Sunday.
to bleed our anguish over the tombstones,

at a much cheaper rate, even though still
at the highest price of the deceased.

They optimistically call this heroes' acre,
yet those other undiscovered heroes
in their watery or unmarked graves
are too numerous for such a small lot.
They are enough to fill a corner of heaven.

Let us, however, refrain from asking:
What are the most deserving grounds
for interring these precious heroes' bones?
Let us think of the heroes' acre
not as a corner in an obscure place
but as fresh and fertile ground,
pullulating with more heroes to come.

For these, I can assure you, are not the last,
nor is this the last we'll hear of heroes.
The minds which machinated their deaths
live still, are with us, amongst the bereaved.
The hearts that stopped theirs from beating
are still driving their Benzes and BMWs,
conceiving more horrors, terrors, and deaths.

IV. Burial of the Bones

As we straighten the lining of the shrouds,
covering our complicity in these deaths,
let us strangle our teardrops emptying
copiously the hollowed eyes and cheeks.

As we iron out our complacency,
throwing handfuls of grief into the hole,
let us cool the guilty soil with wreaths,
and remember the ones that could not be here.

Let us refrain from asking unkindly:
What is this kind of wood
of the coffins we bury them in?
Let us just lower the bones gently.

V. Beyond Hero-Bearing Age

It is an ancient cemetery. this heroes' acre.
It has seen many an old body and bone.
It has enjoyed numerous *zikumbutso* or *sadaka*.
Yet the earth never grows big in fecundity.
Thirty years of overfeeding crocodiles
have not impregnated the drought-stricken land.

The Earth Mother is now famine-ridden.
No juices secrete from her dugs.
Look how her emaciated breasts
hang pendulous like sausage fruit.

Now that she has brought home her children,
let us not ask the usual pertinent question:
What did these heroes die of, or for?
Nor the corollary: Did they have to die?

Let us consider instead an unusual question,
inspired by the old sages: Do these bones live?
Do these exhumations and repatriations
provoke us to re-examine our consciences?

These bones that we have replanted:
Will they take root, sprout, and flower?
What young ideas will spring up
from these ancient graves and bones?
What type of tree will grow here,
nourished by repatriated dry bones?
Will it be the usual graveyard tree, *nkhadzi*,
weeping white sap staining the cemetery,
but offering little or no shade to the inmates?
What is left of these bones to nurture
in a woman who is beyond hero-bearing age?

The Politics of Potholes

I

Come to Malawi and marvel
At the meandering motorways
Leading you to Africa's paradise,
As vistas of natural beauties
Crunch under your screeching wheels
Or are reflected in craters and potholes.

Abandon the Gehennas of the streets,
The pullulating pavements of the cities,
Checkered with patchworks of repairs,
Where the vendors shout plastic prices
And urchins whisper the cost of *chamba*
Or the nearest motel for a quick round.

There are no road signs to warn you
How near the next pothole will be,
Only the roadmap says five hundred.
But do not count like the padre
Tells his beads at prayer time
How many you have survived today.

A model map of smiling Malawi
Unfolds right under the windscreen
And you start your map reading
As the tour of the warm heart begins.

You recognize the knobbly mound there
As the majestic Mulanje Massif.

You confuse the continuous craters,
Thinking they are Chiweta or Chikwawa
The long depression must be the lake.
In the rainy season even the fish
Migrate upland to the giant craters.
You can fish for *chambo* or *kampango*
Without leaving the comfort of your car!

II

Come to Malawi, the warm pothole
Of wildest and roughest Africa.
Tarmac disappears under your wheels
As your squealing and tortured brakes
Mingle with your mouthed ejaculations.
Even the little kid with the toy car
Lifts it from one jagged rim-of-crater
To another murderous edge for safety.

The detonation of your new sump
Is not caused by an itinerant mine.
It is only a bolder left overnight
By some forgetful or disillusioned thug.
The air hissing is not from ripped tires
But your strained pulmonary pumps
As they let out their tired relief
On surmounting yet another big one.

The snaps you hear are not the fan belt,
Flywheel, or even the timing chain.
But your nerves going one by one.
The twinges you feel are not blockages
In the transmission but kilos of adrenaline
Bursting and flooding the bloodstream.
The shuddering is not from the chassis
But your teeth chattering in sympathy.

Forbearance, fortitude, and foresight
Are the only bulky items to carry,
To be declared as excess baggage
At the next road block, as the cop
Waves you on: Keep moving!
He has no patience with survivors
Of craters or potholes in transit
Only the drug pedlars and smugglers.

III

This is Malawi where by-elections
Are held over craters of potholes.
Candidature is marked by the dexterity
On negotiating bumps, holes and craters.
Winning votes is merely by the number
Of potholes contained in your constituency.
Malawi, where defections develop
Over who possesses the biggest craters.
Factions flaring up by claiming ownership
Through dubious ancestry and clanship

Due to the proximity of the potholes.
The local inhabitants can only think
At the rate of twenty kilometers an hour.
But such is the magnitude of their hearts
And the liveliness of the imagination
That over the craters rumor and gossip
Travel at a hundred kilometers per hour.

Due to the buffetings of the long drought
The platitudes of their political slogans
Are so desiccated they are transparent.
But such is the brevity of their memories
They are dreaming of the last régime.
Singing the praises of the first demagogue.
Now they are thinking of reinstating him.

Due to the ravages of extreme poverty.
The only cures for their alleviation
Are bribery, corruption, and seduction,
But such is the warmth of their hearts
They believe that this is the meaning
Of democracy that had been denied them
The last three decades of dictatorship.

The inhabitants suffer from multiple symptoms.
Myopia is rampant: That is why the roads
Just lead to potholes in their potbellies.
But such is the vastness of their pockets
A day never passes without another scam

Involving millions of currency, but affecting
The minions that are also the masses.
Such is what the media misinforms us.

The natives suffer from the AIDS syndrome.
HIV is so positive in each pothole dipped
It comes out dripping with STDs and viruses.
But such is the sturdiness of their dipsticks
And pachydermous the linings of the holes,
The participants believe they'll live forever
In the bliss of their oblivious euphoria.
So won't you please come to Malawi?

Modern Advertising

"Wake up to the world of Leonex"

The song gyrated across the mind
Elbowing out reality
Pirouetted onto the corners of the soul
Bounced against the walls
And curtsied to a crash of cymbals.
It landed outside
And parrot-like chanted to the world:
Leonex! Leonex! Leonex!

The soul erosion exorcised truth
And replaced it more permanently with:
"Life is richer with Leonex!"

Now I use Leonex after-birth lotion-
Thanks to Leonex.
Wash my brains in Leonex liquid.
Thanks to Leonex.
Gargle my soul with Leonex mixture.
Thanks to Leonex.
And dry my tears on a Leonex towel.

The cleansed spirit yearns for the big name:
Life is indeed better with Leonex!"
As I walk down the street

Breathing rarefied Leonex air
And see other Leonex faces
I give my thanks to Leonex.

Gravemates

We meet again at the same
graveyard, familiar grave-mates.
The mounds like tumors of grief
on the ground's face separate us.
Misty eyes moisten the dust storms
raised by the shovels and hoes
refilling the freshly dug hole.

Today it is Tatha's turn.
Yesterday we mourned Malizani's end.
His bougainvillea wreaths are still fresh
as if watered by frequent tear drops.
Last week it was Ndatsalapati.
His flowers are yet less shrunken
than his brothers' and sisters' before him.

Head heavy with haunted thoughts,
we retrace our steps, eyes locking
and glazing over the question:
When shall we meet again:
In laughter, sorrow, or in pain?

The New House

We came home to this:
Rats scuttling under the ceiling,
Cockroaches pullulating in the pantry,
Fruitflies hardened against the cold
Multiplying in the refrigerator.

We came home to this:
Owls' mating calls on the roof,
Claw-tops skidding on the corrugation,
Nightmares chasing each other
On our pillow jolting us awake.

We came home to this:
*Mamba*s slithering in the backyard,
Scorpions connecting across doorways,
Guard dogs dying of rat poisoning.

Between the kitchen and the bedroom,
Between the births and the burials,
Between the spaces created by the silences,
We have to build in our own time
A new home we came to, you and I.

Formula for Funerals

The formula required is not mysterious:
a few famines, droughts, and pestilences;
one or two *napolos* and HIV/AIDS, also,
to control pollution, create depopulation,
and make room for more burial grounds.

The anguish of the bereaved gashes
the sunken flesh of cheeks like gullies
left on the land in the Great Rift Valley,
as tears gush out of eyelashes and sockets
enough really to refill the lake of storms,
razing to the skin any moles and pimples
flash-flooding poles and flattening the hairs
or uprooting them in the wake of their passage.

The lamentation of the mourners furrows
the foreheads like the combined contours
of the Shire Highlands and the Kirk Range
as sorrow terraces the drained temples high
enough to cause the envy of the *mwera*
yet sufficiently deep to be hiding places of
Mulanje, Zomba, Viphya, and Nyika mounts
when the heart's heaviness rises to the head.

Indeed, only a few ingredients are required:
the *mfecane,* slave trade or the *mchape*

and one or two world wars in between
to mobilize spears, poisons, and explosives.
The results make more room for grave mounds.

Who Is Responsible?

("Kamuzu's Grave in Ruins"
The Nation, 8 November 2000, p. 3)

A cenotaph of all cenotaphs
was built in the center of Heroes' Acre
by solemn presidential decree.
In this cenotaph was interred
the life president of all dictatorships.
Around this cenotaph heavy security
paraded and brooded day and night.
But, mark this, that was once upon a time.

The newsman nosed about responsibility:
Who tends to cenotaphs now in Heroes' Acre?
Why the desertion of the camping guards?
Who gave instructions for turning cenotaphs
into ruins so soon after the burial ceremony?

"It's not for us," said the security spokesman,
"to explain the withdrawal of the guardsmen.
It's in the hands of other powers that be:
the Ministry of Home Affairs, for example;
talk to them, they can answer that."

"It's not for me," negated the former minister
for Home Affairs and Internal Security:
I've changed portfolios since then.

I'm now in a different ministry altogether.
Talk to the chairman of the Heroes' Acre."

"I'm not the right person," chided the chair.
"I am out of the Committee for Heroes' Acre.
I'm no longer in government, even,
I'm in the legislature, which is different.
Talk to someone who is able to comment."

The newsman wondered who to turn to next:
The city assembly? The national parks?
Someone surely issued instructions somewhere,
for the lights around the cenotaph are off,
the security men's tent empty and draughty.

Meantime the cenotaph still sinks lower
lamenting over the weight of abandonment;
gathers mold and insomnia of desertion,
weeds and shrubs tickling it over the ramparts,
as nature reclaims the corner into a forest.

Meanwhile more promises and decrees
wrapped in oily rhetoric are dispensed:
a project here and an appeasement there;
a scam here and a cabinet reshuffle there.
Everywhere fiascoes by someone responsible
as everyone scrambles for power or position,
being busy to be the next worthy candidate
fit to be in a cenotaph in Heroes' Acre

Mlauli's Musings

Mlauli said he had foreseen
all these happenings before;
and indeed his predictions
came to be, in our life time.

I

The fields will no longer be ravaged
by locusts because they're radioactive.
Instead the army worm will invade
and eat away the hearts of the stalks.
Fake fertilizers will be fed to the soil
making fools wonder why there's famine.

Rivers and lakes will be exhausted
or emptied because of over-fishing.
Jungles will be silent because of poaching;
forests will be bare because of burning.
The air will become foul for breath,
the water poisonous because of pollution.

Commodities will not be home-grown
but imported at great expense
so that local produce soars in price,
thus enriching the man across the border
as we do our shopping by mail order
or fly to our neighbors to buy our stuff.

II

The youth will no longer be initiated
by the riverside or in the bush shacks
but from sitting rooms watching videos
soon to be banned for explicit pornography
when the watchers know really
what goes on in bedrooms or resthouses.

Public exams will no longer be private
but secretly photocopied and then sold
in the streets, bars, and even school rooms
by teachers arbitrarily transferred or not paid.
And still the man will convene committees
To find out what's wrong, why low standards.

Ministers, MPs, and even entire cabinets
will in broad daylight siphon off funds
meant for the common good or the masses
into their own private accounts or companies
and the man will become so myopic again
to ask for evidence of more proof of corruption.

III

We will no more be afflicted with
common infections like syphilis but
Acquired Immune Deficiency Syndrome.
This we will pass onto our offspring
out of love for each other's partners,
until we learn to stop illicit sex.

Limbs will not sprain walking in gardens
nor bones break falling in bathrooms,
but be mangled by maniacal minibuses
snarling round corners meeting us head-on
with our saloons, cycles, and scooters
or in derailment, crashes, or flounderings

As much as we die from engineered war
or genetic manipulations gone wrong,
we will still multiply at a rapid pace:
huts will be emptied because of poverty,
concrete houses be filled by the unemployed,
and pavements made impassable by vendors.

Mlauli had seen all these events before,
and many more terrifying ones to come.
These, indeed, will also come to pass soon.
It had been decreed and will not be diverted.

Zomba Mountain

Great grandfather, founder of the clan,
baskets of spirits under each arm
claimed your slopes for our village.
We spread between the green banks
of two rivers: Naisi and Naming'azi,
planted and reaped in the fields,
played and prayed in the forests.
hurted and hunted, lived and loved
under the giant gaze of your granite face.

I, too, laden with a packetful of poems
under each arm, staked my claim
on your plateau, peaks, pools, and all,
to wrest the wisdom of the ancients
from the myth-infested forests and rivers.

I read your visage like verse:
savored your similes,
mined your metaphors
wrapped in the roaring rivers
or buried in the bowels of boulders;
deciphered symbols of import
in crag, cranny, or crevice;
scanned cliffs clad in clouds
or rain-laden for fresh inspiration.

Now, great grandfather resurrected
would not recognize your visage.
They blasted your boulders down,
smashing myths to smithereens.
They graded your undergrowth,
mashing water-maids under wheels.
They pulverized the wood spirits,
flattening out their sighs and songs.

Napolo no longer bursts the banks
of Naming'azi, Satemwa, or Naisi;
no myths meander down Mulunguzi;
no lore slithers down the Likangala
past paw steps of lion, leopard, or lizard.
They all vanished into the valley below.

Now the crows fight ants over leftovers
of crumbs of cake from the cottages,
or canned beef, beans, or bottled water
from the backpackers on the camping site.
Concrete, steel pipes, plastic, and bricks
sprout in banks, boulders, and pathways.

Still, the cliffs cleave the skies,
split the sunset into shafts
of red, orange, purple, and blue
doing a dying dance on your brows
sending the slopes to early sleep,

blanketing the town and villages below
in a premature foliage of darkness.
This you will never surrender to man.
This my great grandfather would recognize.

Jerusalem! Jerusalem!

(The International Poets Festival, March 1993)

I. Arrival: Kufika

Tel Aviv garlanded itself bright
from the armpits of the stratocruiser.
The grey wings combed the sky
and there, below us, the lights
twinkled yellow, orange, and red;
then darkness again as we braked
on asphalt and the lights flashed
right under the belly of the bird.

The first glimpses of the stone city
were from the sockets of the land cruiser
swishing on asphalt sweeping the streets
between the poles and splashes of light
clustered like tendrils on the hill slopes
as we curved up and down the valleys
to stop, disembark, and be greeted with:
"Welcome to Jerusalem!" on a card.

II. Shalom! Mtendere!

Shalom! yet the Jewish skullcaps
could not mask the muzzles
of the AK47s strapped
to civilians' backs guarding the kids
by the doors of the synagogue
nor those sightseeing at the windmill.

In the rain some eighteen-year-olds
with machine guns race each other
pounding on the stone pavements
to catch the next train
to the ceasefire line:
Shalom! Peace to you all!

III. Salaam Aleikum! Mtendere!

The bomb exploded outside
and the metaphor in my mind
shattered on the white paper
reluctant to congeal into a poem.
Salaam Aleikum! *Mtendere!*

I walk out of my room
on rubbery legs to meet
an Arab youth with wires
attached to an explosive device
and a tense, hate-filled face.

IV. Penitential Rites: Kulapa

I kneel by the Holy Sepulcher:
Yahweh, you recognize these wounds
the cross made on my soul
since the Old and New Testaments;
the incisions on the heart
since Livingstone's travels.

I gripped the Dome of the Rock:
Allah, you recognize these scars
the crescent made on my psyche
since the Koran and the gun
depopulated my lakeside kin
for white and black ivory
of the old Maravi Kingdom.
Chauta forgive you all!

V. Crossing the Jordan: Kuoloka Yolodani

I squatted on the banks of the Jordan
washed my hands and face
in the cool and cleansing waters,
baptizer and baptized in one.
The waters flowed serenely past me.

My insides ululated to the skies
as I snaked down the Jordan river
and walked across the sea of Galilee:
a cleansed spirit, a new man:
east, west, north and south had kneaded me.

VI. Napolo International: Napolo Kunja

Mlauli roared on Mt Zion:
"Mphirimo! Mphirimo! Mphirimo!"
The blast soared over Mt. Moriah,
hovered in the Gibron valley,
climbed through the garden of Gethsemane,
and perched on the Mount of Olives:

"Kudzabwera Napolo!"
The echo whirled over the Judean desert,
cracked the walls of Jericho,
vaulted over on to the slopes of Mt Gilboa
and rebounded on the Golan Heights.

VII. Departure: Ulendo

The shekel hovered over the hillsides
the olive trees, relics, and tombstones;
sniffed around the Arab, Jewish, and Christian
quarters and left the old city for the new
but did not cross the departure lounge.

The rand, ground in gold,
flew *lugdiens* down the Nile
and Limpopo before the diamonds
and silver took over, like the ground crew,
and we had yet another change of planes.

VIII. Welcome: Takulandirani

I gargled my lacerated psyche
as my soul soared over 30,000 feet
at nine hundred miles per hour
in an ancient Air Malawi
"Takulandirani!" You are welcome!

The Kwacha floated over the farms,
the tea, coffee, and tobacco estates,
the immigration counter, and was home.
The rand, shekel, and dollar were no more.

IX. Home: Kumudzi

Back to the land of *kalilombe*
singing death songs on ruined shrines,
slumbering pythons and drought stricken souls,
locusts, road blocks, army worms, referendums,
to Chingwe's Hole where Napolo was stirring.

I appeased my turbulent ancestral spirits
and spoke to my own people in tongues:
"Shalom! Peace to you, Manchichi!
Salaam Aleikum! and you, Nkhoma!
Mtendere kwaonse amafuno abwino!"

112

Pyagusi

(James Frederick Sangala, Founder of the Nyasaland African
Congress)

I

You were another chameleon
Wearing different names, too,
Like *Nanzikambe*, *Tonkhwetonkhwe*,
Birimankhwe, or even *Kalilombe*.

You were "Pyagusi" the performer,
"J.F." to those who revered you,
And Mr Sangala to those unsure of you:
Politician, businessman, counselor in one.

Whether Chinangwa Farm or Kaphirintiwa,
Your homes were the same: refuge or shrine
Taking in an orphan here, or paying out fees there,
Naming a child here, or arbitrating a dispute there.

Now you survive only in consanguinity:
"Malume," avuncular ties to some,
"Baba," paternal links to others,
"Ambuye," grandfather to them all.

II

They no longer mention you
In these days of instant politics,
Obliterated by heady multipartyism
And the bitter-sweet taste of democracy.

113

They did not mention you even then
At the advent of the first independence,
Obscured by incipient African despotism,
Flung into the wings of deluded nationalism.

Kamuzuism, pseudo politics, broke your back.
And you retreated to Kaphirintiwa
The birth place of all mankind
And, I would say, the African Congress.
You lie in St Michael's and All Angels, your Church.
They should have built you a monument
Called Mute Martyrs of Dictatorship
And All Related Victims of Bandaism.

A Nation of Corpses

We inherited a country of corpses
Not financial losses or devaluations.
We reel under the flotation of cadavers
Not of the Kwacha or the Tambala,
As we auction off coffin-loads of dead.

Exchanging the number of lately dead
Is now the local currency, as we enter
The AIDS victims' figures in our forex
To be wired to international aid organizations
For our foreign reserves to accumulate.

We got rid of the pollution of dictatorship
But let loose pestilences on the population.
Now itinerant HIV and cholera demand
A corpse or two from each household
Not the notorious party card of old.

We do not need Napolo or Phalombe disasters.
We survived those, and the army worms, too,
And the crocodile farms for political dissidents.
Our *awiro* are now overfed, bloated *nalimvimvi*
Welcome terminal cases to the graveyards.

Fateful footsteps pound the corridors
To meet empty offices vacated temporarily
For an appointment with a *mchape* doctor.

Swirling dust storm are not raised by dancing feet
But hurried departures to *rendez-vous* with death.

When it is not funeral bearers we meet
Rebounding on the potholes of our tarred roads,
It is grave-scarred faces we encounter
Returning from spirit-ridden medicine men
Brewing concoctions over the polluted village air.

When truckloads of retuning mourners
Meet in head-on collisions with busloads
Of funeral goers, the excess dead cannot
Be buried in the usual mass graves anymore,
Not when we can export the cadavers.

Our national annual budgets are computed
With the lucrative trade in the corpses
With our less fortunate foreign neighbors
Across the border for their medical colleges.
This is part of our poverty alleviation program.

Advice to Mbona the Prophet

When you visit us again
Through your medium, Mlauli,
Eyes almost popping out
Mouth white with saliva
Voice hoarse with the import
Of what you have to prophesy,

Do not turn your back on us
When we say we know already
The message you bring to us.

There will be drought, you shout.
There is one already in our midst
As devastating as the one last year.
Even the sacred pools are now dry.
You can count the cracked crab-shells
Lying at the bottom of the caked moss.

There will be famine, you cry.
You can see the hundreds dying
Like falling leaves in late summer
Emaciated gray skins peeling off;
Ribs sticking out like unfinished rafters,
Mass graves, we open them every day.

There will be pandemics, you scream.

This is no greater news, really, we say,
What with the cholera victims joining
The AIDS and HIV positives in our midst,
After the malaria compounded with meningitis.

There will be pestilences, you yell louder.
But this comes belatedly to the survivors
Who used to eat the red locusts before.
But the new army worms are not digestible,
Ensuring that punishment comes double-fold.

Spare us your prophetic madness, Mbona,
Convulsive fits and penitential flagellations
All stating the obvious truth invading us,
Living in our midst and decimating us
As we will spare you the only libations left,
Since we can no longer afford the flour.

Speak instead of a world without dread
Though we cannot imagine
What we would be like
Without our familiar afflictions.

The Lasting Flute

No, he was not a relic of the past
Too reluctant to be discarded after
Shaping the new and scrapping the old

Not the long lost *bande* on the beach,
Trodden by heels, sinking into the sand,
Washed further and further away
From the searching eyes of the owner.

Nor was he a new-fangled horn
Fashioned from the castor oil tree
The music to be warped by wilting
In the heat of the new multipartyism

Nor the green river grass flute
Played by the sycophantic youths
In the heady atmosphere of the newly
Discovered democratic ideals and politics,
Only to be whirled away as chaff
After the empty rhetoric has dissipated.

Nor the unfortunate melodious singer,
Hidden in a drum to be touted round
By the itinerant musician of old,
For the audience to do a jig or two,
Forgotten when he departs from them.

He was the lasting flute of bone
Salvaged from the wings of the nightjar
Who, although he lost the smoky contest
Against the clever, conniving tortoise,
Still plays melodies on top of the plateau
Where the ancient *kalilombe* also sings
Her eternal death song at parturition;
Where Changula also howls to hail
Another visit of the dreaded Napolo.

Letter to Mchona

First, we greet you, our son,
with a fat *moni* and smiles
splitting our mouths wide
and filling out each cheek.
If you are well we are pleased,
and hope you will receive this,
one of our several letters,
with the same patience
and calm as we keep on writing you.

Second, the words from our hearts
are not many, we just wanted
to share them with you again.
The ancients said: He who pinches
your ear is a good neighbor, indeed.
How can it not be so, son of our loins?
In spite of your continued silence
we shall not tire writing to you,
hoping for a response in the end.

Third, sad news to shed your tears:
Apasani, your nephew, passed away.
We buried him beside your niece.
We hope you got our telex last week,
since they say this is a quicker way
to send messages than the letters
we sent you of Ndatsalapati's death,

and Zione's demise even before that.
The deaths these days are reckoning
our lives; it is through them we keep track.

Fourth, Atani started having convulsions
They got so bad we asked the *sing'anga*
to have a look at her condition
before she, too, leaves us forever.
He prescribed the *matsoka* for her.
You know what it means: the spirits
of the departed are tormenting her.
We danced and danced and danced for her.
She danced, too, till she fell into a trance
and the spirits spoke through her:
They need *sadaka*, these dearly gone.
It's time they had a feast of the dead.
They won't stop haunting little Atani
till the living remember the forefathers.

Fifth, Zapita, your magnificent bull,
is now a grandfather of several young ones.
It is now two generations since you went,
but he is now thin and wasted with age.
He is rheumy and sleeps most of the time.
It is a marvel he produced at all.
It is of him we write this letter:
He has to be killed for the feast of the dead.
The spirits of our forefathers demanded it.
We cannot deny them their rights.

We hope you are not going to be difficult
about this matter and the one below.

Sixth, you also know Atani is your cousin.
She was your betrothed even when you
went away for these several rains.
You left her just before she was born.
She has now seen several moons too.
She fell to earth last month at last
We danced the *chinamwali* for her.
Then she started having these visions.
At other times she is an ordinary girl,
well behaved and quite dutiful, too.
She should make an adorable companion.
It is time you returned and claimed her.

Seventh, we intend to have your wedding
At the same time as the *sadaka* above.
What is more becoming than to have
the seer of visions wedded to you
on the feast when we welcome our dead.
You, too, are coming from the dead.
It's been so long we won't recognize you.
What is more fitting than to come then?
One who was dead coming with the real dead
and feasting on the bull you left us.
It should make the grand feast of feasts.

Eighth, Sizimpita, your brother in town,
said our letters have had no answers
in the past from you; since the telex
we sent you had no response, too,
we should try to fax you this letter.
And if that should fail, try the e-mail.
But your brother forgets one thing:
We villagers don't know what an e-mail is
though your brother knows what it is.
However, we can't even fax or e-mail you:
Sizimpita doesn't know your addresses there.

Ninth, we are going to post this letter
hoping it will reach you in good time
for you to attend your wedding at least.
Meantime: What is you mining company's
Fax and e-mail for faster communication?
Your brother couldn't find them in the book.

Tenth, when we reach this point, our son,
it means we have finished the letter.
Those are our words. We have already
greeted you. Stay in good health.

The Artists' Cenotaph

Prologue

I arm myself with the mountains,
the mighty massif of Mulanje peak,
the granite face of Zomba plateau,
the undulating flanks of the Nyika.

I wash my soul and body clean
with the waters of the Shire and Ruo,
Mulunguzi, Linthipe and Lilongwe,
Lingadzi, Bua, Rukuru, and Songwe.

I wear the garments of the *kalilombe*,
don the camouflage of her lineaments.
My eyes swell with welling tears,
my chest churns out lamentations.

May this song exorcise the souls
and excise from our spirits the anguish
of the *aluso* languishing in temporary graves,
all awaiting final repose at the artists' cenotaph.

Building the Cenotaph

The artists' cenotaph is in Nyakalambo,
built out of the bones of dead artists,
built for *mlakatuli* and the *mmisiri*,
dedicated to *apalu* and all *alembi*.

This corner of the fabled forest of old
houses all the dead *aluso* of the land,
so why should our lately dead artists
not join the ancient artificers too?

The stone and woodcarvers of the land
labored here for days, weeks and months,
chipping, adzing, scraping and polishing
from the foundation to the high roof.

The python slithers round the flanks,
licking all the corners to shiny smoothness.
The head rears tall and mighty at the top,
as high as the spirit-ridden Sapitwa.

The sturdy ribs intertwine and interleave
with dancers and drummers around a shrine
overgrown with *njale* and *nsangu* trees;
on every leaf perches a *machete* bird.

On every branch hangs a *kalilombe*,
her tail curled round a giant obituary
written by all the artificers of the land;
her hands hold dirges, elegies and laments.

Candidates for the Cenotaph

Chiromo, child of *chiarascuro,*
your blood spattered by the roadside
as the school of *impasto* impacted,
shivered, shattered and starred on tar.

126

hChiwalo, your heart was larger than
your body as you pumped your mighty
GMPG hand on stage and on radio—
the man of many parts really is no more.

Chisiza Jr, deceased so suddenly,
as if you had a contract with death,
to scrap the last of inspiration so early.
Your journey ended at dolorous death's door.

Yekha, the blind troubadour of the south,
you're not so lonely: you have followers.
Madolo, the doyen of the funny flute,
your tunes float to humor us no more.

It is for you the cenotaph was built,
to rest in peace with kindred spirits.
Stars stand aside; shine and stare at
this magnificent monument to genius.

Epilogue

We gathered kindred spirits from afar,
paid homage to the shrines of the north,
bathed our feet at Msinja in the centre,
washed our hands at Ndione in the south.

Makewana gathered her kindred deities too,
Mwali, Salima, Chisumphi and Chiuta.

Not to be left out were Napolo and Chiluwe,
akumidima, akumatsoka, and *akumizimu.*

We sang symphonies of the spheres
as we ringed round the artists' cenotaph,
and the *aluso* sang back to us in tongues:
WE ARE NOT DEAD! OUR WORKS LIVE ON!

Street Seller's Song

The first shower spits down
on the sizzling pans frying chips
to ambush the unwary buyers
going home hungry at knock-off time:
      the builders and the shop assistants,
      the messengers and the bus conductors,
      the petrol attendants and the watchmen.

The street seller's shout drowns
the spattering drops of rain escaping
through the gashes of the plastic roof
as his commerce goes up in steam,
sorrowfully folds up his wet wares
of silk, wool, and cotton from far-off lands
in the west via the east wrapped in bales:
designer suits, winter coats, thermal underwear
from anonymous donors presumed dead.

Sodden hopes spring from sunken eyes
viewing the soaking exotic merchandise
affordable only at the month end,
what with the devaluation of the currency.
Meantime he drenches his financial progress
at the tavern selling stale opaque beer
to the blasted music from holed speakers.
No credit card or certified checks required.

As the street seller sips his first drink
the week passes by in quick review:
getting up at the chill hour of dawn,
a baleful walk to the grass stand
by the bus or train station in town;
off-loading, spreading, stacking, or dusting
under the shed sagging like a scarecrow;
watching the march of the morning feet:
>   the cleaner, the waiter, the doorman,
>   the laborer, the maid, the mechanic,
>   the carpenter, the woodcutter, the clerk.

Eyes careering at the feat of chauffeurs
missing the cyclists by a cloth-breath;
marveling at the tinted cars carrying
anonymous big shots in back seats
from the suburbs labeled low density,
maximum security residential areas;
marble three-bathroomed mansions
with private swimming pools in the gardens:
>   the lawyers and the executives,
>   the managers and the brokers,
>   the doctors and the accountants.

Coming home late to the woman partner
also in the petty trading business in town,
she, too, stops by the kill-me-quick tavern
for a drink or two and more of the same;
fortifying herself for the walk back home

of daub and poles and plastic off-cuts,
with the roof held down by broken stones;
where roaches run from the rats
running from the geckos
running after the mosquitoes
breeding in a nearby effluent-laden stream,
where the weekly washing is done
while the children splash about after school run by:

        the priests and the nuns,
        the reverends and the bishops,
        the brothers and the sisters.

Both the street seller and his partner
are united in sips and in thoughts
as they view the coming season:
the rains are a disservice to street selling.

The Cry at Birth

(Dedicated to fetuses)

What baby at birth wouldn't cry,
Plopping into the world only to inherit
Shingles, Kaposi's sarcoma and HIV/AIDS?
Or doomed to be abandoned in festering dustbins
Or to be swimming in worm-infested latrines?

What baby at birth wouldn't strangle
Itself with its own umbilical cord,
Destined to be raped or sodomized by
Its own lusty father at six months?
Doomed to have its reproductive organs
Ripped off for medicinal concoctions?

What baby at birth wouldn't drown
Itself in its own after-birth waters,
Orphaned at day one by AIDS parents,
Fated to be lame, blind, mute, or insane,
To roam the hungry and indifferent streets
In a country devastated by famine and drought?

What baby at birth wouldn't choke
The second it started breathing the air
Ready to explode with global warming?
Ordained to drink from the city sewers

Chock-full with piss, shit and condoms
Or fetuses that didn't survive as he did?

What baby at birth wouldn't retch,
Predestined to see the myth-infested forests
Burnt down by man on the rampage?
Or lakes poisoned, gardens invaded by army worms?
Destined to dine on mad-cow diseased beef
Or migratory birds infected with avian flu?

What baby at birth wouldn't prefer
Asphyxiation to death by the atomic bomb
Chemical warfare or terrorist suicide killers
Or mental derangement due to drug abuse
Or *napolo* flash floods, *el niños* or the *tsunami*
Or face a lynch mob, murderer, or the gas chamber?

What baby at birth wouldn't wail or whimper,
scream or screech, groan or moan?
What baby, tell me, would still be determined
To come out or live at all in this world?

Just Before One for the Road

Across the counter my irritants
Sheath their smiles by sipping:
They don't want to splash me
With their bleary glances.
Someone strangles a guffaw
Like you wring wet hands
Before greeting a stranger.

Disco music pummels eardrums
Leaden decibels cave them in
No mosquito dare float in
For fear of being ricocheted back
Through the vibrating burglar bars.

The stomps on your toes are signs
That you are not alone on earth.
The prostitute's distress signals
Are lost in a swirl of thoughts
Perhaps, if her thigh keeps on pressing
Something will give way—perhaps.

A prospective customer replaces
A glass with another, afraid of refills
Potential airborne viruses park
On unsuspecting but willing victims.
The prostitutes' freewheeling feelers
Reach their mark and settle insistently.

Fluorescent lights spark glittering passion
Between slinking yielding flesh embracing
Before heading out for a sleazy quickie.

Nachifukan Man Left No Traces

(He lived and died 10,000 BC)

Nachifukan man left no potsherds
No cave paintings of his hunting
Whether or not he fought battles.
There are no bones to tell his tales
Of his life or the giant creatures:
Reptiles or mammals, his neighbors
Or what actually killed him in the end.
He just vanished and became extinct
He left no birth or death certificates
His story is a closed book going unread.

Archeological man probed the puzzle
Perched behind his electronic gadgets
In air-conditioned laboratory museums
Shone laser lights on his dark days
Trying to piece together Nachifukan man:
What he must have looked like
What he must have lived like
But there wasn't even any dna left.
No relics to put on the display shelf
He just came and demised silently.

I can't then be at odds with my past
When I can't find my ancestor's ruins;
When he bequeathed me no monoliths.

I can't wipe my memory clean of him
When he didn't leave me any mementos;
When he didn't leave me any monuments
So what right has my mysterious ancestor
Got now to claim me as his descendant?

Morning at Mvuu Camp

Honking hippos serenade the camp
throughout the teeth-chattering night.
Moonlight and starlight spiral down
and dance on the shimmering Shire.

The motor boat knifes the grey waters
at dawn, delivering early visitors
and waking up a chorus of crooning
from fretful and fluttering feathers.

The chill of the July dawn defies
the double blankets and body heat
to pluck sleep from frozen eyelids.
Wakefulness thaws receding dreams
as goose pimples sprint across skin
and reactivate shivering limbs.

Yet, in the ragged rents of the clouds
the peeping blue promises pleasant weather
over the misty mantle and dew grass
across the ripples, reeds, serge and trees;
and resident warthogs, lizards and hippos.

Operational Corpses

We must take stock of our corpses.
Weigh their coffins and gauge
their worth in our *memoriam*s.

The village head casts a shadow
that does not rise higher than a tombstone
even the grave trees overshadow it.

Prancing Pyagusi, founder of the NAC
deserves more than a city graveyard
when his followers are in the hero's acre.

Warm memories waft over Chilembwe
generating his own remembrance day
for a revolution that rocked a colony.

The memory chills over Kamuzu's bones.
Cold marble mourns over his mausoleum
built for the demagogue of all times.

Handling only a meager budget the memory
cannot retrieve rain priests and priestesses whose
shrines are now overgrown with national amnesia.

A Writer's Desk at Sixty

(On being given a custom-made writer's desk as my 60th birthday present)

I

This writer's desk speaks of sixty seasons

More solid than the surprised recipient.
Wood from the sturdy sausage tree
Smoothened like the balding poet's pate,
Its bulbous fruit matching his bulging belly,
It will last the poet beyond his sixth decade!

This sausage tree desk suits the owner,
He of the *mombo* brachystegia family,
The multipurpose builder's tree of old.
Gnarled and knotted trunk all planed,
Yet retaining the curls and contours.

II

You are no mass-produced chief's chair
With ready-made motifs to boot:
Hyenas howling on luxurious leaves,
Leopards lounging on forked branches,
Long-tailed monkeys chattering away,
Sleek leonine shapes slinking to streams,
Target for tired tourists at street corners.

You are a custom-made artist's delight.
Craftsmanship gleams in the joinery,

Pride pours out of the planed planks
Looking like the water-licked sides
Of a seasoned canoe at the seashore.

You are poetry in wood hand-delivered
To the melodies of the local music band,
Flanked by supportive relatives: parents,
Sisters, brothers, cousins, nephews and nieces;
Friends: lawyers, doctors, academics, pastors
And aspiring writers like this sexagenarian.
No politics, only the sheer sense of sharing.

III

You are the perfect set for a sexagenarian,
Coming with the matching upright chair.
The see-through "C" carved into the back-rest,
A personalized symbol saying indelibly:
Here sits the writer hitherto licensed to create.

By his side is the indispensable waste bin,
In the same wood and just as curvaceous
With its gnarls, knots, and slopes asking:
Is this where discarded inspiration retires?

No, this is not the end or burial of the muse.
Just as the tree was luxurious with fruit,
Just as the poet was productive in youth,
The next decade promises multivarious works,
A transmutation of inspiration and wonders.

See the old pine desk secreted to the computer office.
It only bore coniferous fruit and needles for leaves.
The exotic tree joined the new electronic media,
Replaced by this indigenous tree in the old study,
Earthed by gems of ancient lore and legends.

Exit the writing desk of the green days
Pullulating unbridled inspiration and creativity.
Enter sagacity, discretion, and maturity.
I now wear the sights of the seer's muse.

IV

See, gone is the multi-drawered desk,
Wherein went writing pads and notebooks,
Pens, pencils, rubber bands, string, pins,
Business cards, envelopes, stamps, tapes,
Disks, sharpeners, sellotape and prestik,
Files, photos, films, and folders,
Cuttings – pending, to be classified,
Scribblings – pining to be expanded,
Even insects coffined in glass cases.
Now welcome to multi-layered shelves,
Hardwood pencil holders and their trays,
Sliding into their own grooves at the top.

Yet in the euphoria of the 60th birthday
The same old artefacts haunt me:
The stained scissors and stapling machine.
Do my fragments of memory look so antique?
The octogenarian puncher and card-holder.

Do my innards resist renewal like this?
The antediluvian pencil sharpener and 12-inch ruler.
Why do I retrieve debris from the old desk?
They look like mementos of imminent death to me!

V

The accretions of the not-to-be-trashed stuff
Mingle with the plastic receiver and cords,
All creamy white, and the telephone directory,
All yellow, squatting on the pristine desk.
At least the smell of varnish on dry wood
Will not vanish entirely from the study.
It will seep into all inspiration therefrom,
Ooze out of the muse's flights of fancy,
And persist into the dreams of the old poet,
Licensed at last to write at sixty.

The sixty decades that have now gestated,
Forty of them were spent in courting the muse.
This decade, seemingly speeding startlingly,
Sutures the past experiences and inspirations
Into, as it were, a ceaseless frenzy,
As if afraid it could be the last.

Usayelekele Mine

Usayelekele Mine is not mine,
But you can buy me,
And of course the mine,
At the affordable price
Of deforming my children,
And, if any, my grandchildren,
With radioactive waste.

There is this political party.
Like the mine, it has to go on.
That's what is really at stake.
In fact, it is an investment of his,
To be remembered in his afterlife.
It is no big deal, to tell the truth,
Where they dump the waste.

The radiation is a slow time bomb.
You don't feel it in your lifetime.
My conscience was auctioned off
Like the NGO's, chief's, or minister's
Mis-molded by international self-interests,
Who, deep down, are also mine-holders,
Reluctant to be mere sleeping partners.

I'm a past master in willful genocide,
Strategic planner in corpse manufacture,

Internal auditor in deadening opposition,
Expert at muzzling mediocre minds,
Fertilizing lapses in institutional memory,
Aware of Activities Against Development,
And late-stage genealogical cul-de-sacs.

My previous posts and achievements:
Depletion of the lake fish,
Because I liberated the waters;
Deforestation of the mountains,
Because I condoned wood cutting;
Pollution of the ozone layer,
Because I permitted gas manufacture.

Usayelekele Mine is my latest challenge,
I bring to it my vast vacuous experience,
Activated intellectual bankruptcy,
Blinkered myopia and double dealings.
Currently I'm majoring in obfuscation,
Sustainable disinformation, and moneymaking.
My thesis: to make this an explosive package.

And Now, Our Honorable MP

He went on about the moral fabric,
About the politicians, how corrupt,
Insensitive, and self-serving they were.

The government departments, the scams,
In industry, the frauds and double-dealings,
And the entrepreneurs turned millionaires.

How the churches had gone all commercial,
The clergy become daylight moral transvestites,
The academics mute and failed the country.

How the thugs were castrating the men,
Or dismembering the women in the bushes,
And the trials leaving the perpetrators free.

How the wives were castrating the husbands,
The husbands dismembering their spouses,
And the spouses raping their young offspring.

And how it was in their days when still young,
When at independence or even first republic,
Or say colonial period, things were different.

Those Beggars on Fridays

You can view them on any Friday
Walking, limping, slouching into town
From nowhere on calloused feet,
Gnarled hands at shop doors,
Being spouted again to the next one.

The gray-haired old dodderer
Carrying a patched spotted head,
A grimy bag over a hunched shoulder.
The skinny scarred woman
Walking crabwise on the road,
The shrunken sockets glowing,
As if holding imprisoned liquid.
Several blind with knobbly hands,
Led by bedraggled boys and girls.
They look like giant pairs
Of grounded flying ants,
In their upright positions.

The resident beggars have staked
Their territories on street corners.
The bedraggled woman at the filling station,
With a brood of kids climbing over her,
Or raising dust a few feet away.
The polioed man with shrunken arms
And knees showing through tattered patches,

His modified bicycle parked by the bridge.
The wizened denizen bent double
Greets you in broken English at the bank,
A quivering suggestive hand outstretched.
The malnourished girl, skin folded over,
The thin scabied arms and spindly legs,
Plying her trade by the Post Office.

The street kids prefer the covered verandah
Of the supermarkets, carrying customer's goods.
There's more money and dignity in doing that.

The Last Hitch Hike

a coffin-load
of lingering images
carries
the sweet pods of life
hanging on
by the tendrils.

a few reluctant images
are flung
to land on the roadside
and roll
into the open ditches:
cul-de-sac

and other
bottled experiences
race past
only to branch off
at the T-junction
or halt at the sign:
road closed.

have you been served?

a cosmetic smile revealed
pearls cloistered by
glistening lip-ice
overhung by vibrant nostrils
capped by the mane of a wig

radar vision
piercing the roots
of my being

rolling twin hills
imprisoned by clinging
playtex

ebony bust
charging
nerve endings.

Song of the Loincloth

history covers the *nyanda* with false humiliation
imported feelings delivered in a white c.o.d. package
labeled: exotic western complexes ready-made
sophistication and values made-to-measure
designed in Britain, tailored in Russia and packed in the U.S.
paid for as an intellectual piece of ritual protection
against perception of reality and truth
which lie flaccid in three-piece suits bell-bottoms and minis.

at least in my *nyanda*
in my *nyanda* I said
I can stand proudly erect
toying with the hard truth
rearing its head in the face of slimy lies
trumpeting to a shallow wilderness of mutes.

a piece of *nyanda* like the truth is dangerous
(it should be kept locked in chests!)
it exposes strange not-to-be-revealed-in-public forms
columns of lies flowing into deltas of cloying nests
meandering into hairy thickets of words:
the outgrowth of a lie bisected by a central truth

it lies hidden between parted lips
anticipating tickling fancies and fabricated lies
languishing and caressed by the *nyanda* only

and excited into orgasmic eruptions by a truth
ejaculated and mercilessly penetrating
releasing and exposing what lies underneath
the *nyanda* and the verbal circumcision.

Pounding Hymn

'Mamuna upita njiramo dzatenge
thwack! dzatenge! thwack!'

The mango tree dwarfs
womankind bowing and rising
below as though in ceaseless
supplication to her god.

'Ngati ufuna mutuwu dzatenge
thwack! dzatenge! thwack!'

The rising pestle momentarily
eclipses a ripe mango
then plunges again into
the gaping hole of the mortar.

'Ngati ufuna mkonowu dzatenge
thwack! dzatenge! thwack!'

Brown arms grip brown pestle
rising and falling in timeless rhythm
jogging ripe bare breasts
of the woman chanting behind.

'Ngati ufuna beleli dzatenge
thwack! dzatenge! thwack!'

The orange tip of the mango disappears
again on brown as the nipples
of suppliant breasts rise to acknowledge
the tree god standing erect above.

'Ngati ufuna thakoli dzatenge
thwack! dzatenge! thwack!'

The smooth roundness of the mortar
swells with the repeated assaults
of pestle head plunging
up and down and up again.

'Ngati ufuna mwendowu ndakana
thwack! ndakana! thwack!'

The god sighs gently in the wind
turns his face away from womankind
as the seed spills from the lips of the mortar
and cackling hens come to peck their fill.

Poetry Power

(For the late W.M., Lecturer at Chancellor College)

We met in a demilitarized zone,
A public place for p-leisure, you and I,
Drink in hand and cigarette between lips.
It was just an ordinary confrontation.

But just a month ago in the same place,
It was not a common ground for pleasantries.
You met a colleague of mine, too, here.
We buried him a few days later, sadly.

Your meeting with my colleague here
Was lethal: he did not survive it.
It was so devastating for him and us:
Some broken ribs and other internal injuries.

You said: the public needs education
On how to behave when they encounter grenades.
You were prepared to conduct workshops.
How best, you asked, could you go about it?

I said you need more education
On how to respond to ordinary civilians,
Meeting in neutral zones in peacetime,
Like a bar, dancing floor, or restaurant.

Somehow we could not communicate.
You were making a valid point of survival.
I was defending defenseless civilians,
And you wanted us to fight it out.

Yet my weapons are only words and sentences,
Couched in pleasing combinations or contours,
To produce mellifluous cadences of music
To delight the ear and educate the emotions.

Your weapons are AK47s, landmines, and grenades,
Manufactured in munitions factories
To produce cacophonies of bullets or shells
To deafen the ear and deaden the emotions.

My field is literature, pullulating with words.
I wade through similes, metaphors, symbols,
To produce the essence of things or beings,
The real, deeper meaning of existence,

Your field is warfare, populated with guns.
You wade through rural or urban terrain
To produce the death of the populace
Or the end of civilization, so to speak.

I am trained in the art of verbal warfare:
Repartee, innuendo, ambiguity, irony,
How to communicate with maximum impact
For the betterment of civilized mankind.

You are trained in the martial arts:
Riposte, guerrilla warfare, military tactics,
How to destroy so there's no retaliation,
So you can emerge the ultimate hero.

We parted without physical combat.
I went my own way to the next disco,
You went yours to the next battlefield,
Somehow pleased there were no casualties.

A Word on Poetry

Poetry
invigorates after
assaulting you out of the lethargy of apathy
          and complacency
paralyzing with the terror of the unexpected
probing into the rusted joints of the mind:
          oiling as it scrapes
tantalizing with an elusive image
          writhing on its head
flagellating to
          a yelp of pain
          a snarl of anger
          a squirm of uneasiness
          a smile of satiety
          a moan of a heart stroked to tautness.

Poetry
rejuvenates after
leading to "a hairy thicket of words"
galvanizing nerve endings to a quivering
          mass of anticipation
inviting tactile exploration where the
          other senses are feeding
erecting even the hairs on their toes to
          violent participation
leaving you spent and gasping faintly:
          "no more—not just yet.

Printed in the United States
by Baker & Taylor Publisher Services